Practice for Book 7C

Contents

CAMBRIDGE
UNIVERSITY PRESS

CAMBRIDGE UNIVERSITY PRESS
Cambridge, New York, Melbourne, Madrid, Cape Town, Singapore,
São Paulo, Delhi, Dubai, Tokyo

Cambridge University Press
The Edinburgh Building, Cambridge CB2 8RU, UK

www.cambridge.org
Information on this title: www.cambridge.org/9780521537926

© The School Mathematics Project 2003

First published 2003
4th printing 2010

Printed in India by Replika Press Pvt. Ltd.

A catalogue record for this publication is available from the British Library.

ISBN 978-0-521-53792-6 Paperback

Typesetting and technical illustrations by The School Mathematics Project
Illustrations on pages 48–49 by David Parkins
Illustrations on page 113 by Chris Evans
Cover image Getty Images/Randy Allbritton
Cover design by Angela Ashton

❷ Symmetry

Section B

1   Some of the dotted lines on these designs are lines of symmetry.
    Some of them are not lines of symmetry.
    Which of the lines are lines of symmetry?

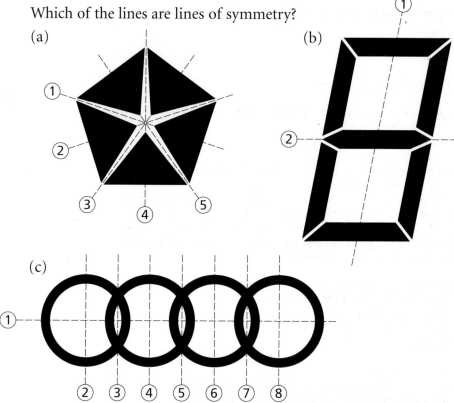

(a)

(b)

(c)

2   (a) How many different ways can you
        shade two squares in this 3 by 3 grid
        so that it has two lines of symmetry?
        Sketch the different ways.

    (b) Sketch the ways for a 4 by 4 grid.

    (c) Do the same for a 5 by 5 grid.

Section C

1 Which of these designs have rotation symmetry (of order greater than 1)?

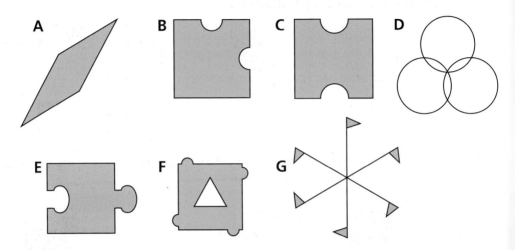

2 For each design, find the order of rotation symmetry.

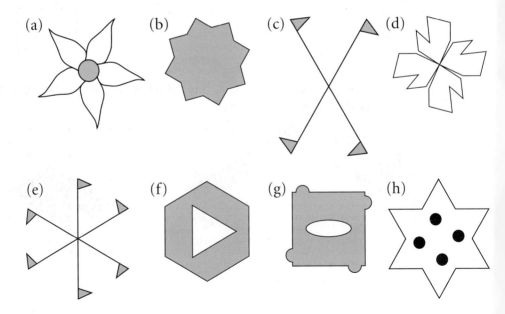

Section D

1   Copy and complete each design so it has rotation symmetry of order 4.
    Each centre is shown by a large dot.

(a) 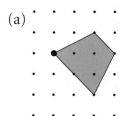   (b) 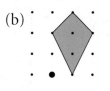   (c) 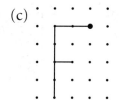   (d)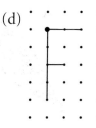

2   Copy and complete each design so it has rotation symmetry of order 2.
    Each centre is shown by a large dot.

(a) 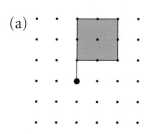   (b) 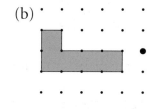   (c)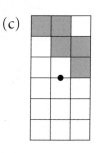

3   Copy and complete each design so it has rotation symmetry of order 3.
    Each centre is shown by a large dot.

(a)   (b) 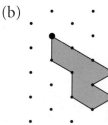   (c)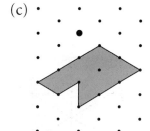

Section E

1 Many of the walls of the Alhambra Palace in Spain are covered with
   tiling patterns. The diagrams below show some of these tiles.

   Describe the symmetries of each tile.
   (For example, 'The tile has no lines of symmetry. It has rotation
   symmetry of order 2.')

(a)

(b)

(c)

(d)

(e)

(f)

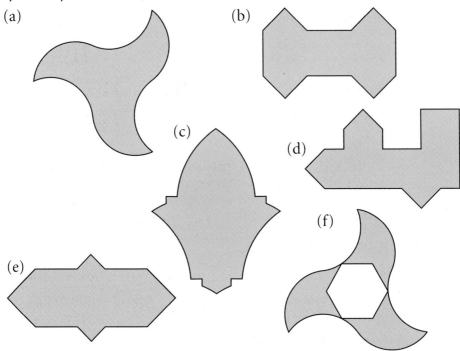

2 Describe the symmetries of each domino or card.

(a)

(b)

(c)

(d)

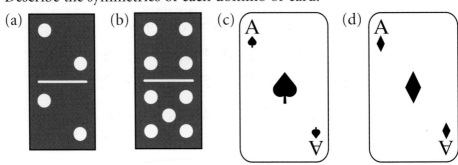

Section F

1 Some years have a line of symmetry when they are printed, for example **-1381-**

(a) Which of the years below have one line of symmetry?

(b) Which have two lines of symmetry?

(c) Which have rotation symmetry?

1961	1881	2002	1331
1066	1991	1301	1811
1812	1521	1380	1691

2 List as many years as you can between 1800 and 2000 that have either reflection or rotation symmetry.

3 Some addition sums have a line of symmetry:

-8-+-3-=-11-

Find some addition sums of your own that have a line of symmetry.

4 Here is a multiplication with a line of symmetry:

-181-×-10-=-1810-

Find some more multiplications with a line of symmetry.

5 (a) Which of these capital letters have rotation symmetry?

A B C D E F G H I J K L M
N O P Q R S T U V W X Y Z

(b) The three-letter combination **OZO** has rotation symmetry. Write down some four-letter combinations with rotation symmetry.

Section H

These are the shapes of some pieces from a computer game called 'Tetris'.

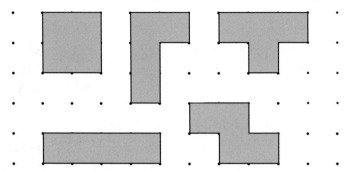

1   Copy the diagrams.
    Describe the symmetries of each piece.
    Mark any centres of rotation and show all lines of symmetry.

2   This shape is made from two T-shaped pieces.
    They do not overlap.

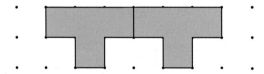

    Describe the symmetries of this new shape.

3   Use two T-shapes with no overlapping to make
    (a) a shape with rotation symmetry and no reflection symmetry
    (b) a shape with both rotation symmetry and reflection symmetry

4   Choose one of the other Tetris pieces.
    With two or more of your shapes, try to make a design with
    (a) reflection symmetry but no rotation symmetry
    (b) reflection symmetry and rotation symmetry
    (c) rotation symmetry of order 4

③ Number skills

Section B

1   Match each calculation to the correct result.

    24 × 36   58 × 63   14 × 46

    38 × 14   28 × 24   46 × 36

    532   864
    644   1656
    672   3654

2   Work out the total value of each sheet of stamps.

(a)

39p	39p	39p	39p	39p	39p	39p
39p	39p	39p	39p	39p	39p	39p
39p	39p	39p	39p	39p	39p	39p
39p	39p	39p	39p	39p	39p	39p

(b)

43p	43p	43p	43p	43p	43p
43p	43p	43p	43p	43p	43p
43p	43p	43p	43p	43p	43p
43p	43p	43p	43p	43p	43p
43p	43p	43p	43p	43p	43p
43p	43p	43p	43p	43p	43p

3   Find the missing digits.   (a) 34 × 23 = ▥8▥

                              (b) 27 × 3▥ = ▥37

                              (c) 72 × 1▥ = 1▥68

4   Use just these four digits.
    Use all of them to make two 2-digit
    numbers (for example, 45 and 27).
    Multiply the numbers together.
    Show how to make

    (a) the largest possible result

    (b) the smallest possible result

    (c) the result that is closest to 2000

5   56 and 57 are a pair of consecutive numbers.
    So are 312 and 313.
    Find a pair of consecutive numbers that multiply to give 702.

Section C

1 For my birthday party I want to buy 33 paper hats.
   The hats come in packets of 5.
   How many packets must I buy?

2 I also need to buy 33 plastic spoons.
   The spoons come in packets of 10.
   How many packets of spoons will I need?

3 I was given 28 creme eggs for my birthday.
   I put the eggs into boxes, with 6 eggs in each box.
   How many boxes did I fill completely?

4 I need to put 130 sausage rolls on to plates.
   Each plate holds 8 rolls.
   How many plates will I need to use?

5 6 boys share £5.70 equally. 8 girls share £6.80.
   Who gets more, each boy or each girl?

6 4 friends pick apples. They pick 37, 43, 29 and 44 apples.
   They decide to put them together and share them out equally.

   (a) How many apples do they each get?

   (b) How many more do they need to pick to avoid
        having any left over?

7 Sadia and her friend need 180 litres of water to fill their pond.
   They takes water to the pond in buckets which hold 8 litres each.
   How many bucketfuls will they need?

8 John is making concrete.
   To fill his mixer he needs
   6 buckets of gravel, 4 buckets of sand and
   2 buckets of cement.
   He has got 117 buckets of gravel, 83 buckets of sand and
   49 buckets of cement.
   How many times can he fill his mixer?

Section D

1 Work out each of these and give the remainder (if there is one).

(a) $157 \div 12$ (b) $205 \div 16$ (c) $368 \div 32$ (d) $199 \div 17$

(e) $555 \div 43$ (f) $401 \div 23$ (g) $500 \div 22$ (h) $387 \div 14$

2 Lidcup Scouts organise a trip to London by coach.
454 people want to go.
Each coach holds 64 people.
How many coaches will they need?

3 18 friends do the Lottery each week. They each pay £6.

(a) How much do they pay altogether each week?

(b) One week they win £414 and share it out equally.
How much do they get each?

4 Lemonade bottles are put into crates to go on lorries.
Each crate holds 24 bottles.

(a) How many crates can you fill with 500 bottles?

(b) How many crates do you need to put 650 bottles on the lorry?

5 This sheet of stamps costs £6.08.
What is the value of each stamp?

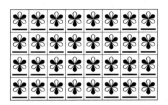

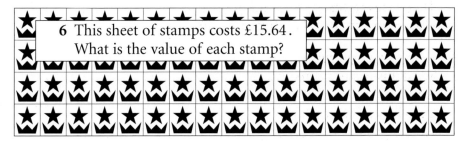

6 This sheet of stamps costs £15.64.
What is the value of each stamp?

Section E

1 I need 200 computer discs.
They come in boxes of 24.

    (a) How many boxes will I need to buy?

    (b) How many discs will I have spare?

2 Sarah thinks of a number.
She multiplies it by 35.
Her answer is 980.
What number did she think of?

3 Jay has 820 bricks.
He puts them into 23 piles, with the same number in each pile.
He has 15 bricks left over.
How many bricks are in each pile?

4 There are 517 people coming to a concert.
The seats can be put out in rows of 24, 28 or 32.
Which size row will give the smallest number of empty seats?

5 When Jody shares out her collection of rings between her 6 children,
each child gets 35 rings and there are 4 rings left over.
How many rings does Jody have?

6 Pip has some apples.
When he puts them in 2 piles there is 1 apple left over.
When he puts them in 3 piles there is 1 left over.
The same happens with 4, 5 and 6 piles.
What is the smallest number of apples he could have?

7 When Karl shares £300 equally between his grandchildren,
there is £1 left over (they each receive a whole number of £s).
When he shares £400 equally between them, there is £10 left over.
How many grandchildren does Karl have?

Section F

Use a calculator for these.

1 Find the remainder when
  (a) 1000 is divided by 7   (b) 10 000 is divided by 70
  (c) 4321 is divided by 79   (d) 1234 is divided by 129
  (e) 9999 is divided by 87   (f) 1 000 000 is divided by 333

2 A whole box of 72 computer mice costs £300.
Separately, the mice cost £5.50 each.
A company wants to buy 2000 mice.
What is the cheapest way for the company to buy the mice?
How much will the mice cost altogether?

3 Josephine has over 1000 postcards.
When she takes out 21 of them she can arrange the rest
into 12 equal piles.
When she takes out 12 of them she can arrange the rest
into 21 equal piles.
What is the smallest number of postcards she could have?

4 When I divide 892 by a certain number the answer is 27,
with a remainder.

  (a) What number did I divide by? (b) What was the remainder?

5 Find the missing numbers a to g.
  (a) When 284 is divided by a, the result is 18 remainder 14.
  (b) When b is divided by 26, the result is 14 remainder 9.
  (c) When c (between 800 and 900) is divided by 31,
       the result is d remainder 4.
       (How many different answers can you find?)
  (d) The difference between $\frac{1}{2}$ of e and $\frac{1}{3}$ of e is 15.
  (e) The difference between $\frac{1}{2}$ of f and $\frac{1}{3}$ of f is 28.
  (f) The difference between $\frac{1}{10}$ of g and $\frac{1}{100}$ of g is 45.

④ Growing patterns

Sections B and C

1 This chain of 4 squares has 13 'corners' (•).

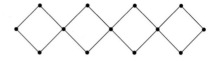

(a) Sketch a chain of 5 squares and count the number of corners.

(b) Copy and complete this table.

Number of squares	1	2	3	4	5	6
Number of corners				13		

(c) Describe how the number of corners goes up as the number of squares goes up.

(d) Explain why the number of corners goes up in this way.

(e) How many corners will there be in a chain of 10 squares?

(f) Which of these gives the number of corners for a chain of n squares?

      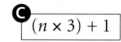

A $n \times 4$ **B** $n + 3$ **C** $(n \times 3) + 1$

2 This chain of 5 overlapping squares has 17 corners.

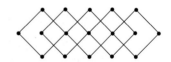

(a) Sketch a chain of 4 overlapping squares and count the corners.

(b) Copy and complete this table.

Number of overlapping squares	2	3	4	5	6
Number of corners				17	

(c) Which of these gives the number of corners for a chain of n overlapping squares?

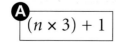   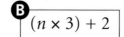   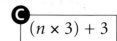

A $(n \times 3) + 1$ **B** $(n \times 3) + 2$ **C** $(n \times 3) + 3$

Sections D and E

1 A 2 by 2 grid contains 5 squares altogether:

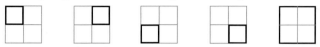

A 3 by 3 grid contains 14 squares altogther:

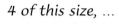   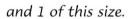

9 of this size, ...   *4 of this size, ...*   *and 1 of this size.*

(a) How many squares are there on a 4 by 4 grid?

(b) Copy and complete this table.

Size of grid	1 by 1	2 by 2	3 by 3	4 by 4	5 by 5
Number of squares		5	14		

(c) Describe how the number of squares goes up.

(d) Try to explain why the number goes up in this way.

2 A rod made with 3 cubes can be broken into pieces

in these different ways: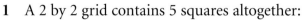

If we include the unbroken rod as well, this gives 4 different arrangements altogether.

(a) How many arrangements are there with 4 cubes?

(b) Copy and complete this table.

Number of cubes in rod	1	2	3	4	5
Number of arrangements			4		

(c) Describe how the number of arrangements increases.

(d) Try to explain why the number increases in this way.

6 Number patterns

Sections B, C and D

1 Work these out.
   (a) 3^2 (b) 7^2 (c) 9^2 (d) 100^2

2 Work out each of these.
   (a) $14^2 - 13^2$ (b) $15^2 - 13^2$ (c) $16^2 + 1^2$ (d) $10^2 - 9^2$

3 Work these out.
   (a) 3^3 (b) 10^3 (c) 11^3 (d) 5^3

4 Work out each of these.
   Then write them in order of size, smallest first.

$$6^2 + 2^3, \quad 5^3, \quad 15^2, \quad 10^2 - 6^2, \quad 4^3 + 4^3, \quad 10^3 - 9^3, \quad 3^3 + 6^3$$

5 Anna has 2000 multilink cubes.

   (a) She arranges as many as she can in a square.
       How many multilink cubes are there in the square?

   (b) She uses as many cubes as she can to build a big cube.
       How many multilink cubes are there in the cube?

6 Without using a calculator, write down the square root of
   (a) 16   (b) 49   (c) 4   (d) 144   (e) 400

7 The population of Texas is 16 000 000.
   Suppose everybody stood in a giant square.
   How many people would be along each edge?

8 The time for a complete swing (to and fro) of a pendulum depends
   on how long it is. A rough formula is
      time of swing in seconds = 2 × $\sqrt{length\ of\ pendulum\ in\ metres}$

   (a) How many seconds does it take a 1 metre pendulum to swing?

   (b) Roughly how long would the swing of a 10 m pendulum be?

Sections E and F

1 What is the rule for working out the next number in each of
   these sequences?

   (a) 34, 45, 56, 67, 78, 89, ...   (b) 34, 28, 22, 16, 10, ...

   (c) 5, 15, 45, 135, 405, ...   (d) 480, 240, 120, 60, 30, ...

2 Write down the next number in each of the sequences in question 1.

3 This sequence of patterns is made with matchsticks.

  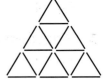

   (a) Count the matchsticks in each pattern and write down the
   first three numbers of the sequence.

   (b) Sketch the next pattern and write down the next number
   in the sequence.

   (c) What is the connection between this sequence and the sequence
   of triangle numbers?

   (d) Explain the reason for this connection.

4 Look at this table.

   Answer the questions below without continuing
   the table yourself.

   (a) Which number will be in the 17th row and
   2nd column?

   (b) Which number will be in the 52nd row and
   3rd column?

   (c) In which row and column will these numbers
   be?

      (i) 146   (ii) 247

1	2	3	4
5	6	7	8
9	10	11	12
13	14	15	16
17	18	19	20
21	22	23	24
25	26	27	28
29	30	31	32
33	34	35	36

Angles and triangles

Sections A, B, C and D

1 Draw a triangle whose sides are of length 3 cm, 4 cm and 5 cm. Measure and record its angles.

2 Explain why it is impossible to draw a triangle whose sides are of length 3 cm, 4 cm and 8 cm.

3 Which, if any, of the four triangles in this diagram are

   (a) isosceles

   (b) scalene

   (c) equilateral

   (d) right-angled

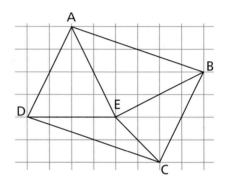

Section E

1 (a) Draw accurately the triangle shown in this sketch.

   (b) Measure and record angle C and the lengths of the sides AC and BC.

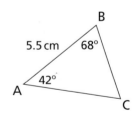

2 Draw accurately the triangle shown in each of these sketches. Measure and record the remaining sides and angles.

(a)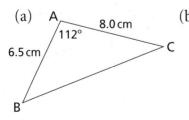

(b)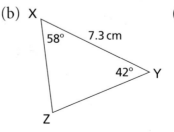

(c)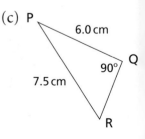

Section F

1   Work out the angles marked with letters.

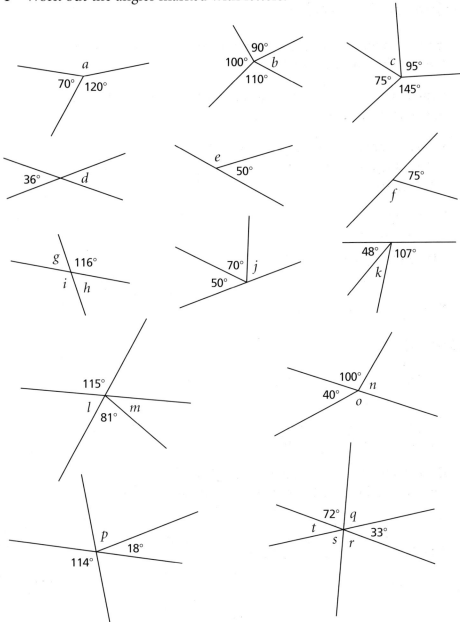

Section G

1   Work out the angles marked with letters.

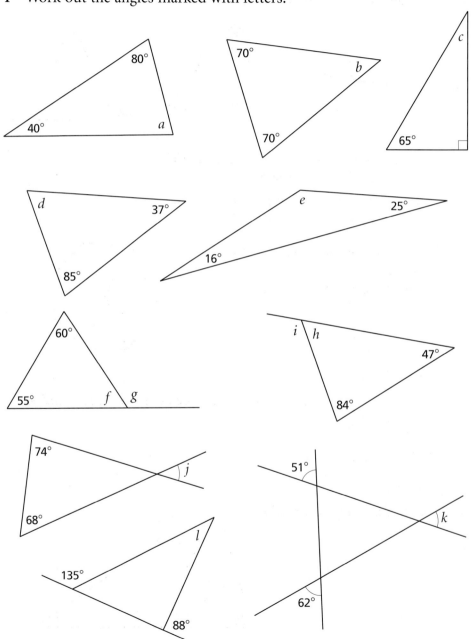

Section H

1 Work out the angles marked with letters.

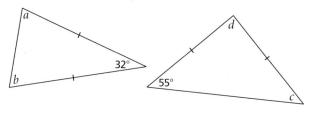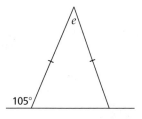

2 (a) One angle of an isosceles triangle is 130°.
What are the other angles?

(b) One angle of an isosceles triangle is 50°.
What could the other angles be?

3 The diagram on the right shows a
regular octagon.
Calculate the angles *a* and *b*.

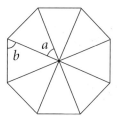

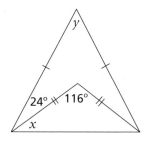

4 Calculate the angles marked *x* and *y*.

5 Calculate the angle marked *a*.

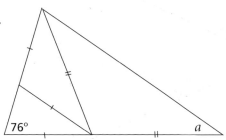

21

Fractions

Sections A and B

1 What fraction of each of these shapes is shaded?

   (a) 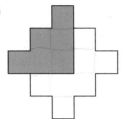   (b) 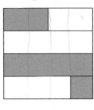   (c)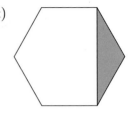

2 Copy these and fill in the missing numbers.

   (a) $\frac{1}{4} = \frac{}{32}$ (b) $\frac{2}{3} = \frac{}{21}$ (c) $\frac{3}{5} = \frac{}{45}$

3 Simplify each of these fractions as far as possible.

   (a) $\frac{15}{35}$ (b) $\frac{25}{40}$ (c) $\frac{15}{24}$ (d) $\frac{16}{80}$ (e) $\frac{14}{42}$

4 Write each of these decimals as a fraction, as simply as possible.

   (a) 0.44   (b) 0.34   (c) 0.04   (d) 0.55   (e) 0.3

Sections C and D

1 Which is the larger fraction in each pair?

   (a) $\frac{2}{3}, \frac{5}{8}$ (b) $\frac{3}{7}, \frac{2}{5}$ (c) $\frac{5}{6}, \frac{7}{9}$

2 Write each of these mixed numbers as an improper fraction.

   (a) $1\frac{1}{5}$ (b) $1\frac{3}{8}$ (c) $2\frac{1}{3}$ (d) $2\frac{7}{8}$ (e) $3\frac{1}{4}$

3 Write each of these improper fractions as a mixed number.

   (a) $\frac{6}{4}$ (b) $\frac{12}{5}$ (c) $\frac{15}{4}$ (d) $\frac{8}{3}$ (e) $\frac{20}{6}$

4 Write these in order of size, smallest first: $\frac{29}{12}, \frac{45}{20}, \frac{36}{15}$

Sections E and F

1 Work these out.

(a) $\frac{1}{4} + \frac{1}{5}$ (b) $\frac{5}{8} + \frac{1}{3}$ (c) $\frac{2}{3} + \frac{1}{7}$ (d) $\frac{2}{5} + \frac{3}{8}$

(e) $\frac{3}{4} + \frac{1}{3}$ (f) $\frac{4}{5} + \frac{3}{10}$ (g) $\frac{5}{6} + \frac{5}{8}$ (h) $\frac{5}{12} + \frac{2}{3}$

2 Work these out.

(a) $\frac{3}{4} - \frac{2}{5}$ (b) $\frac{7}{8} - \frac{6}{7}$ (c) $\frac{7}{20} - \frac{1}{4}$ (d) $\frac{9}{10} - \frac{1}{4}$

(e) $\frac{1}{2} - \frac{2}{7}$ (f) $\frac{8}{9} - \frac{1}{6}$ (g) $\frac{2}{3} - \frac{1}{9}$ (h) $1\frac{1}{2} - \frac{5}{7}$

3 Work out   (a) $4 \times \frac{7}{8}$ (b) $\frac{2}{3} \times 5$ (c) $12 \times \frac{5}{8}$

4 You have these four fractions: $\frac{1}{10}$ $\frac{1}{6}$ $\frac{1}{4}$ $\frac{1}{3}$

Here are some of the ways of adding two different fractions
from the list: $\frac{1}{10} + \frac{1}{4}$, $\frac{1}{6} + \frac{1}{3}$, $\frac{1}{4} + \frac{1}{3}$

Find all the possible results of adding two different fractions
from the list. Write them in order of size, starting with the smallest.

5 You have the four digits 2, 3, 4, 5.
You put them into the four spaces on the right.

(a) What is the largest possible result?

(b) What is the smallest possible result?

6 Repeat question 5 for the digits 3, 5, 6, 8.

7 You have the four digits 2, 3, 4, 5 to put into
the four spaces on the right.

(a) What is the largest possible result?

(b) What is the smallest possible positive result?

8 Repeat question 7 for the digits 3, 5, 6, 8.

9 You have the three digits 4, 5, 6 to put into these spaces:
What is the smallest possible result?

Mixed questions 1

1 Make three copies of this diagram.

With as little extra shading as possible, make the diagram have

(a) two lines of reflection symmetry

(b) rotation symmetry of order 2

(c) rotation symmetry of order 4

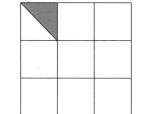

2 Cans of fruit are transported in boxes with 24 cans in each box. Without using a calculator, work out

(a) the total number of cans in 33 full boxes

(b) the number of boxes needed to transport 425 cans

3 In each of these sequences the numbers go up or down in equal steps.
Work out the missing numbers.

(a) 13, 34, 55, ..., ..., ...   (b) 16, ..., 34, ..., ..., 61

(c) ..., 53, ..., 31, ..., ...   (d) 18, ..., ..., 33, ..., ...

(e) 17, ..., ..., ..., 29, ...   (f) 40, ..., ..., 19, ..., ...

4 Calculate the angles marked with letters.

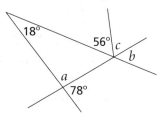
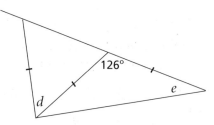

5 Draw accurately a triangle ABC in which AB = 8 cm, angle A = 48° and angle C = 82°. Measure BC and AC.

6 Work these out, giving each result in its simplest form.

(a) $\frac{5}{8} - \frac{2}{5}$ (b) $1\frac{3}{4} + \frac{5}{6}$ (c) $2\frac{1}{5} - \frac{5}{6}$ (d) $\frac{1}{3} + \frac{1}{4} + \frac{1}{10}$

7 (a) What is the order of rotation symmetry of each of these designs?

(i) 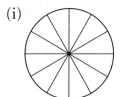   (ii) 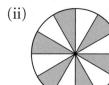   (iii)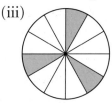

(b) Copy design (i) and shade it so that it has rotation symmetry of order 4.

(c) How many lines of reflection symmetry does each design in part (a) have?

8 A farmer dies, leaving instructions in her will as to how the farmland is to be divided up between her four children.

The eldest is to get one third, the next one quarter, the next one fifth and the youngest the rest.

What fraction does the youngest get?

9 Imagine that this pattern continues.

(a) Which number will be at the end of the 10th row of triangles?

(b) Work out whether the number 395 will be in a triangle like this: $\triangle$, or like this: $\triangledown$. Explain your answer.

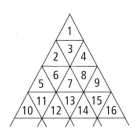

10 Do these without using a calculator, showing your working.

(a) I think of a number.
I multiply it by 14. The result is 364.
What number did I think of?

(b) I think of a number.
I divide it by 17. The result is 23 with remainder 10.
What number did I think of?

⑪ Health club

This table gives information about the members of the Cool Health Club. Use it to answer the questions on the opposite page.

Name	Sex	Age group	Height (m)	Weight (kg)	Swimmer
Alldred, B	M	21–30	1.84	77	Yes
Bharat, K	M	31–40	1.75	65	Yes
Billings, J	F	31–40	1.55	48	Yes
Brent, M	M	41–50	1.82	80	Yes
Charles, W	F	41–50	1.60	52	No
Desai, R	M	21–30	1.79	69	Yes
Draper, P	M	51–60	1.77	81	No
Duval, J	F	21–30	1.48	48	Yes
Fogarty, L	M	41–50	1.84	88	Yes
Hemraj, D	M	31–40	1.76	73	No
Irwin, N	F	31–40	1.51	56	No
Jhupdi, H	M	31–40	1.77	67	Yes
Jobson, S	F	21–30	1.49	46	No
Khalid, V	F	41–50	1.50	52	No
Larson, I	F	31–40	1.63	68	Yes
Mitchell, M	M	21–30	1.85	64	Yes
Morris, J	F	41–50	1.55	51	Yes
Nicholls, B	F	31–40	1.70	64	Yes
Owens, R	M	51–60	1.80	88	No
Patel, S	M	41–50	1.82	71	Yes
Patrick, H	F	41–50	1.69	66	No
Richardson, T	F	41–50	1.65	59	Yes
Teller, G	M	51–60	1.77	77	Yes
Vishram, S	M	41–50	1.79	82	Yes
Woolf, V	F	21–30	1.58	49	No

Sections B and C

1 (a) Draw a dot plot of the heights of the men aged 41 or over.

(b) What is the median height of these men?

2 (a) Draw a dot plot of the weights of all the women.

(b) What is the median weight of the women?

3 This is a bar chart of the age groups.

In which age group does the median age fall?
Explain how you get your answer.

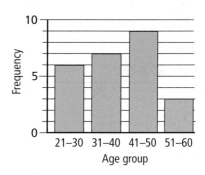

Section D

1 Copy and complete each of these two-way tables.

(a)

	Swimmers	Non-swimmers
Men		
Women		

(b)

Age	Swimmers	Non-swimmers
21–40		
41–60		

(c)

Age	Men	Women
21–40		
41–60		

⑫ Balancing

Section B

Choose a letter to stand for the unknown weight in each of these puzzles.
Write an equation for the puzzle and solve it.
Check each answer.

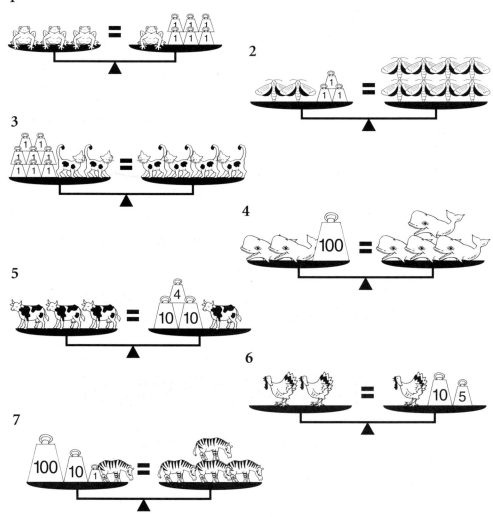

1

2

3

4

5

6

7

Section C

1 (a) Copy and complete the
   equation for this puzzle.

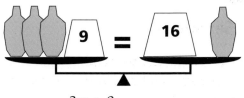

$$3w + 9 = \ldots$$

   (b) Solve the equation and check your answer.

2 Solve these equations.
   Show all your working and check that each answer works.

   (a) $4t + 7 = 2t + 20$ (b) $18 + w = 3w + 6$

   (c) $2m + 17 = 3m + 5$ (d) $50 + 3t = t + 82$

   (e) $10p + 11 = 3p + 88$ (f) $10 + 200x = 1000 + 101x$

3 Solve these equations.
   Show all your working and check that each answer works.

   (a) $0.8t + 40 = 1.1t + 10$ (b) $1.8 + w = 3w + 0.6$

   (c) $20m + 1.7 = 30m + 0.5$ (d) $500 + 3t = t + 820$

   (e) $p + 11 = 0.3p + 88$ (f) $10 + 2x = 1000 + 1.01x$

4 In this picture, each van is 3.9 m long.

   Use c to stand for the length of each car, in metres.
   Write down an equation for the puzzle.
   Solve it to find the length of each car.

⑬ Multiples and factors

Sections B, C and D

1 Goldbach's conjecture says that every even number greater than 4 can be expressed as the sum of two prime numbers.

For example, $10 = 3 + 7$ $20 = 7 + 13$ $100 = 47 + 53$

Find all the ways of expressing these as the sum of two primes.

(a) 30   (b) 100

2 Make factor trees for   (a) 36   (b) 70

3 What are the missing numbers in these factor trees.

(a) 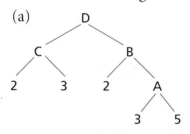   (b)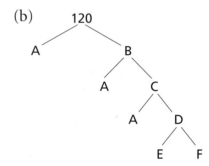

4 (a) Find the prime factorisation of 60.

(b) Use your answer to (a) to find the prime factorisation of 600.

5 Find the prime factorisation of 14 400.

6 Find the missing numbers in these prime factorisations.

(a) $360 = 2^a \times 3^b \times 5$ (b) $756 = 2^a \times 3^b \times c$

7 Find the prime factorisation of each of these square numbers.

(a) 16   (b) 36   (c) 100   (d) 900

(e) What can you say about the powers in the prime factorisation of a square number?

8 Here are some ways of arranging nine different digits so a correct multiplication occurs.

$12 \times 483 = 5796$ $42 \times 138 = 5796$ $18 \times 297 = 5346$
$27 \times 198 = 5346$ $48 \times 159 = 7632$

Use these to find the prime factorisation of
(a) 5796   (b) 5346   (c) 7632

Sections E, F, G and I

1 Find the lowest common multiple (LCM) of
(a) 6, 12 and 15   (b) 12 and 28

2 Write down the LCM of
(a) $2^2 \times 3$ and $3^3 \times 2$ (b) $2 \times 3^2 \times 5$ and $2^3 \times 5$
(c) $3^2 \times 7$, 5×7^2 and 2×5^2 (d) 3^4, $2^2 \times 3$ and 2×5^2

3 Find the highest common factor (HCF) of 48 and 72.

4 Write down the HCF of
(a) $2^2 \times 3$ and $3^3 \times 2$ (b) $2 \times 3^2 \times 5$ and $2^3 \times 5$
(c) $3^3 \times 7$, $3^2 \times 7^2$ and $3^2 \times 7^3$ (d) $2^4 \times 5^2$, and $2^2 \times 5^4$ and $2^3 \times 5^3$

5 Find the HCF of 506 and 1863.

6 Three bells ring at intervals of 18, 24 and 32 minutes.
If they all ring together at noon, when will they next all ring at the same time?

7 Four barrels can hold 72, 24, 56 and 120 litres.
What is the size of the biggest jug which can be used to fill them exactly?

8 A 'palindromic number' is one which reads the same when the order of its digits is reversed, e.g. 272 or 37873.

Which of these palindromic numbers are also prime?

    101   111   121   131   141   151

⑭ Work to rule

Section A

This tile 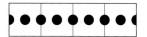 is used to make 'friezes'. Here are some friezes.

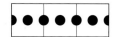
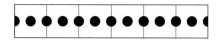

The 4-tile frieze has 7 complete circles. (Don't count the part-circles.)

1 Copy and complete this table.

Number of tiles	1	2	3	4	5	6
Number of circles	1			7		

2 What is the rule for working out the number of circles when you know the number of tiles?

3 Use the rule to work out the number of circles when there are 60 tiles in the frieze.

4 How many tiles are there in a frieze with 85 circles?

Sections B, C and D

1 Find a rule for the number of complete circles in friezes like these.
   Use t for the number of tiles and c for the number of circles.

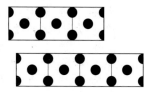
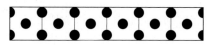

2 This tile 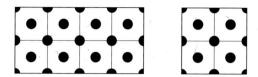 is used to make double friezes.

Find the rule connecting the number of tiles and the number of circles and explain how you found it.

3 Find the rule for each of these friezes.
Explain how you found each rule.

(a)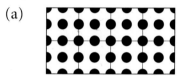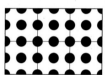

(b)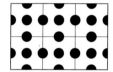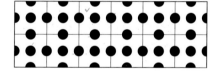

Section E

1 This tile is used to make square designs.

2 by 2 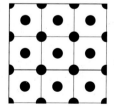   3 by 3   4 by 4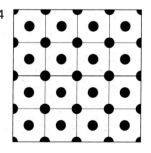

Find the rule for the number of circles in the *t* by *t* design.

⑮ Decimals 1

Sections A and B

1 You can make the calculation | 6.8 | × | 10 | = | 68 |

from these cards. | 10 | 100 | 1000 | ÷ | × | = | 57 | 0.57 | 680 | 68 | 6.8 |

What other calculations can you make from the cards?

2 Write down the answers to these.

    (a) 100×0.065 (b) $18.3 \div 1000$ (c) $2.13 \div 100$

    (d) 0.054×1000 (e) $460 \div 100$ (f) $9.46 \div 1000$

3 Work these out without a calculator.

    (a) 0.3×52 (b) 48×0.02 (c) 160×0.7 (d) 0.04×70

4 What calculations can you make from these cards?

| × | = | 0.08 | 0.5 | 0.6 | 20 | 24 | 25 | 30 | 32 | 40 | 300 | 500 |

Sections C and D

1 Round these to 2 d.p.

    (a) 85.348   (b) 7.1092   (c) 26.0677   (d) 1.4963   (e) 23.996

2 (a) Round 44.2862 to 3 d.p.   (b) Round 4.0854 to 2 d.p.

    (c) Round 0.0196 to 3 d.p.   (d) Round 0.7048 to 2 d.p.

3 Work these out without a calculator.
If the result does not come out exactly, round it to 3 d.p.

    (a) $0.45 \div 4$ (b) $1.37 \div 5$ (c) $5.2 \div 8$ (d) $1.4 \div 3$

    (e) $2.51 \div 7$ (f) $3.39 \div 6$ (g) $8.3 \div 9$ (h) $0.5 \div 8$

Sections E and F

These problems may involve +, – or ×.
Estimate first, then use a calculator.
Write down your estimate as well as the calculations and answers.

1   Before a heating experiment a beaker and its contents
    weighed 88.6 g.
    After heating the beaker and contents weighed 69.3 g.

    Calculate how much was lost during the heating.

2   For £1 Peter gets 9.54 South African rand.
    How much does he get for £280?

3   Peter changes 125 rand to dollars
    when the exchange rate is 1 rand to 0.176 dollars.

    How many dollars does he get?

4   How much do you have to transfer
    from the left side to the right side
    to make these scales balance?

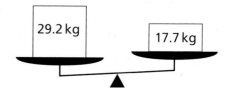

5   Grade A carpet costs £11.85 a square metre.
    Grade B carpet costs £8.95 a square metre.

    Ramesh wants to carpet two bedrooms.
    He needs 11.56 square metres for the large bedroom and
    8.24 square metres for the small one.

    (a) Calculate the cost of each of these options.

        (i) Grade A for both rooms

        (ii) Grade B for both rooms

        (iii) Grade A for the large room and grade B for the small room

        (iv) Grade B for the large room and grade A for the small room

    (b) Calculate the difference in cost between options (i) and (ii).

    (c) Calculate the difference in cost between options (iii) and (iv).

Section G

1 Calculate the unit cost of each of these.
  Write the answer in the form '... per litre' or '... per kg' etc.

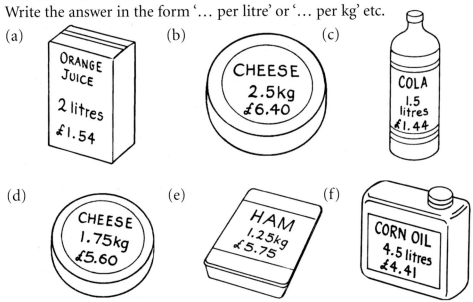

(a) ORANGE JUICE 2 litres £1.54

(b) CHEESE 2.5kg £6.40

(c) COLA 1.5 litres £1.44

(d) CHEESE 1.75kg £5.60

(e) HAM 1.25kg £5.75

(f) CORN OIL 4.5 litres £4.41

2 In each pair below, which gives you more for your money?
  Explain why, in each case.

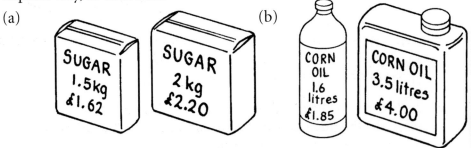

(a) SUGAR 1.5kg £1.62   SUGAR 2 kg £2.20

(b) CORN OIL 1.6 litres £1.85   CORN OIL 3.5 litres £4.00

3 From London to Clacton is 70 miles. The train fare is £19.
  From London to Southend is 40 miles. The train fare is £9.70.

  (a) Calculate the cost per mile for each journey.

  (b) Which journey has the lower cost per mile?

Section H

Show each calculation as well as the answer.

1   If £1 is worth 6.10 Polish zloty, how many zloty are these worth?

   (a) £3   (b) £25   (c) £45.50   (d) £0.70

2   If 1 US dollar is worth £0.80, how much are these worth in £?

   (a) 5 dollars   (b) 38.80 dollars (c) 0.65 dollar

3   Kate sells fizzy orange at a school fair.
   She buys 35 litres of juice at £0.88 per litre
   and 25 litres of fizzy water at £0.36 per litre.
   She mixes them and charges £0.90 per litre for the fizzy orange.

   How much profit does she make if she sells it all?

4   Which of these jars of honey
   is better value for money?
   Explain why.

5   Rajesh came back from a holiday in Brazil with 126 Brazilian reals.
   At the bank they gave him £1 for 2.20 reals.
   What did he get in £ for 126 reals?

6   A shop normally sells dress material at £3.49 per metre.
   In a sale, the price of a 'remnant' (an odd bit left over) is £13.
   The remnant is 4.65 metres long.

   (a) How much would the remnant cost at the normal price?

   (b) What is the cost per metre of the remnant?

   (c) Susie needs 3.50 m of dress material.
       Is it cheaper for her to buy the remnant or to buy 3.50 m at the
       normal price?

Section I

1 Copy and complete this grid, without using a calculator.

Input	÷ 40	÷ 4	÷ 0.4
800		200	
4			
20			
		9	

2 Copy and complete this grid, without using a calculator.

Input	÷ 5	÷	÷ .....
100		2	200
30			
		1	
2000			

3 Think of any number. Write it down.
Will each of the following make it bigger or make it smaller?

(a) × 10   (b) ÷ 100   (c) ÷ 0.1   (d) × 0.1

(e) × 100   (f) ÷ 10   (g) × 0.01   (h) ÷ 0.01

4 Here are six calculations and six rough answers.
Without using a calculator, pair off each calculation with
a rough answer.

(a) 13.7 − 6.8   (b) 18.2 × 0.6

(c) 8.9 × 9.1   (d) 78.2 ÷ 97

(e) 44 ÷ 0.12   (f) 7.8 + 39.1

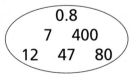

0.8
7   400
12   47   80

5 Dina chooses two numbers from this list
to make a division (for example 1.8 ÷ 6).

0.6   1.8   0.03   2.4
    6   0.2   1.2

(a) Which division gives the largest result?

(b) Which gives the smallest result?

Section J

1 A magazine comes out once a month and costs £1.60.
I can get it every month for 12 months by paying
a subscription of £16.20.

(a) How much would 12 magazines cost at the normal price?

(b) How much do I pay per magazine if I pay the subscription?

(c) The magazine offers an 18 month subscription for £25.
Is this better than the 12 month subscription? Explain.

2 Here are two petrol pumps from
different garages.

A 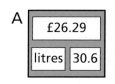 B

(a) Which garage sells the cheaper
petrol?

(b) How much would 20 litres at garage B cost?

3 This table shows distances and ordinary single rail fares from London.

Place	Liverpool	Manchester	Newcastle	Penzance
Distance (miles)	194	184	269	305
Single fare	£92.50	£98.50	£85.00	£77.00

Calculate the cost per mile for each journey, to the nearest 0.1p.

4 A shop has an account card that gives
the cardholder a reduction each time
they spend at least £20 (see table).

Jo has a card.
She wants to buy items costing

£15.35,   £9.89,   £17.48,

£22.80,   £32.60,   £18.30.

Total cost	Reduction
up to £19.99	none
£20–£29.99	£1
£30–£39.99	£2
£40–£49.99	£3
£50–£59.99	£4
£60 or over	£5

If she buys them all together she will get a reduction of £5.
If she buys them separately she will get a reduction of £3.

How should she buy them so as to get the largest reduction?

16 Gravestones

Section F

Colin has made a new kind of fertiliser. He hopes it will make his turnips grow better.

To find out if it works, he plants 60 turnip seeds. When the plants start to grow, he puts the fertiliser on 30 of them but leaves the other 30 without it.

He weighs all the turnips he gets. Here is the data.

Weights of turnips in grams

Without fertiliser

210	287	136	304	219	296	183	197	133	152
208	160	173	124	268	165	180	139	242	178
213	282	163	107	134	150	201	216	166	174

With fertiliser

145	208	159	168	273	261	302	230	285	269
167	243	227	316	338	342	224	133	331	276
220	270	294	318	250	265	308	152	271	316

1   Make two grouped frequency tables, one for each set of turnips. Decide for yourself what groups to use.

2   Draw a frequency chart for each set of turnips.

3   Write down the modal group for each set of turnips.

4   Does the fertiliser give bigger turnips? Explain how you decided.

Mixed questions 2

1 The members of a club were asked to sign up for either swimming or climbing as an activity. Here are the results.

Name	Sex	Activity
Jill	F	Swimming
Craig	M	Climbing
Sven	M	Swimming
Dina	F	Climbing
Will	M	Climbing
Joshua	M	Swimming
Daniel	M	Swimming

Name	Sex	Activity
Paula	F	Climbing
Zeta	F	Climbing
Roger	M	Climbing
Sara	F	Swimming
Grant	M	Climbing
Elaine	F	Swimming
Qahir	M	Swimming

Name	Sex	Activity
David	M	Swimming
Lauren	F	Climbing
Neeta	F	Climbing
Andy	M	Climbing
James	M	Swimming
Petra	F	Climbing
Saul	M	Swimming

Copy and complete this two-way table.

	Swimming	Climbing
Male		
Female		

2 Solve each of these equations. Check each answer.

(a) $3n + 53 = 6n + 26$

(b) $13 + 8n = n + 55$

3 Copy and complete each of these factor trees.
(The two letter Cs both stand for the same number, and so on.)

(a) 240

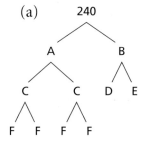

(b) 243

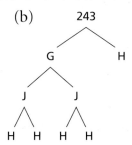

(c) 245

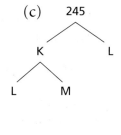

4 Find a rule for working out the number of white tiles when you know the number of black tiles.

Use w for the number of white tiles and b for the number of black tiles.

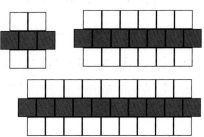

5   Do this question without a calculator.

Three shops, A, B and C, sell Murki bars.

Shop A sells 3 bars for £2.69.
Shop B sells 4 bars for £3.49.
Shop C sells single bars for £1.09 but if you buy 4 you get an extra bar free.

In which shop is a Murki bar cheapest?
Explain how you decide.

6   This bar chart gives information about the ages of the animals in a colony.

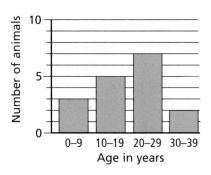

The number of animals in the colony changes only when an animal is born or dies. No animal ever joins or leaves.

Ten years later the bar chart looks like this.

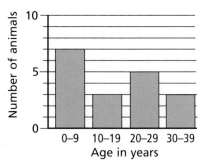

(a) How many animals were born during the ten-year period?

(b) How can you tell that none of the animals aged less than 20 at the start of the period died during the period?

(c) How many animals aged 20 or over died during the period?

Area and perimeter

Section B

In the diagrams below, all lengths are in centimetres and all angles are right angles.

1 Work out the area of each of these shapes.

(a)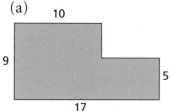

(b)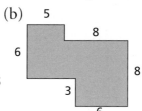

(c)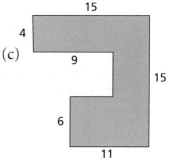

2 Work out the surface area of each of these solid shapes.

(a)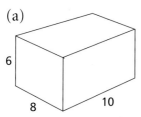

(b)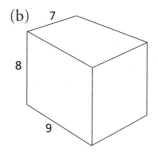

(c)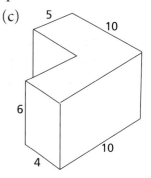

3 How many pieces 5 cm by 4 cm can be cut from a sheet of card 1 metre square?

4 The area of a rectangle is 4 cm². The length is 5 cm. Calculate the width.

5 Jack is painting a white line along the edge of a roadway. He has enough paint to cover 4.5 m².

(a) How many square centimetres are there in 4.5 m²?

(b) If the line is 10 cm wide, how long will it be, in **metres**?

Section C

1   Work out the areas of these right-angled triangles.

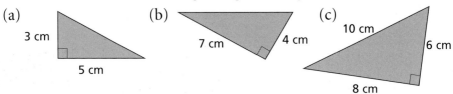

(a) 3 cm   5 cm

(b) 7 cm   4 cm

(c) 10 cm   6 cm   8 cm

2   Work out the area of each of these shapes.

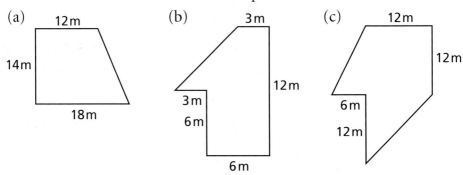

(a) 12 m   14 m   18 m

(b) 3 m   3 m   6 m   12 m   6 m

(c) 12 m   12 m   6 m   12 m

3   Work out the area of each of these shapes.

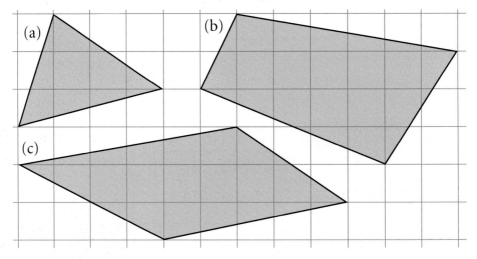

(a)

(b)

(c)

Section D

These questions are to be done without a calculator.

1 Work out the area of each of these shapes.

(a)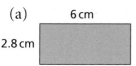
6 cm
2.8 cm

(b)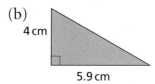
4 cm
5.9 cm

(c)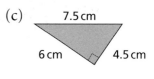
7.5 cm
6 cm   4.5 cm

2 Work out the area of a rectangle with dimensions
(a) 5 m by 3.6 m   (b) 0.5 m by 3.6 m   (c) 0.05 m by 3.6 m
(d) 0.4 m by 2.8 m   (e) 0.2 m by 12.6 m   (f) 0.3 m by 40 m

3 The area of a rectangle is 11.6 cm². The length is 4 cm.
Work out   (a) the width   (b) the perimeter

4 The perimeter of a rectangle is 15.6 cm.
The length is 4.8 cm.
Work out   (a) the width   (b) the area

Section E

These questions are to be done without a calculator.

1 Calculate the areas of these rectangles.
(a) 2.5 cm by 2.5 cm   (b) 3 cm by 5.5 cm   (c) 6.5 cm by 3.5 cm
(d) 1.5 cm by 6 cm   (e) 4.5 cm by 2.5 cm   (f) 7.5 cm by 1.5 cm

2 Work out the area of each of these shapes.

(a)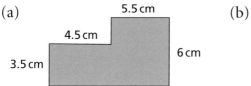
5.5 cm
4.5 cm
3.5 cm
6 cm

(b)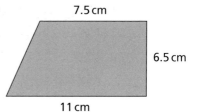
7.5 cm
6.5 cm
11 cm

Section F

Questions 1–3 are to be done without a calculator.

1 Work out the area of these.

(a)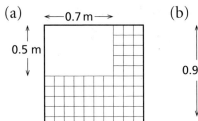

(b)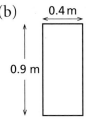

(c)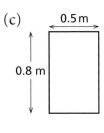

2 What is the total area here?

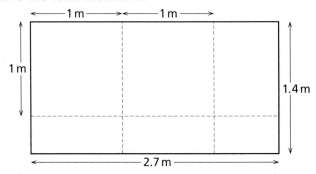

3 Work out the area and perimeter of these rectangles.

(a) 1.5 m by 1.6 m   (b) 2.4 m by 0.7 m   (c) 1.8 m by 1.5 m

(d) 0.9 m by 0.8 m   (e) 7.2 m by 7.2 m   (f) 6.2 m by 0.5 m

4 Make the measurements you need to calculate the area of this shape. Sketch the shape and mark your measurements on the sketch.

Use a calculator to work out the area of the shape.

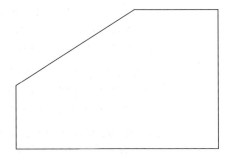

⑱ Negative numbers 1

Section B

1 Write down a calculation which fits each of these diagrams.

(a) 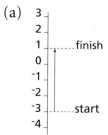 (b) 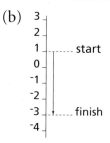 (c)

2 Copy and complete these.

(a) $3 - 6 = ?$ (b) $^-2 - 8 = ?$ (c) $0 - 7 = ?$ (d) $2 - 4 = ?$

(e) $3 - ? = ^-2$ (f) $5 - ? = ^-1$ (g) $? - 3 = ^-10$ (h) $? - 2 = ^-1$

3 Copy and complete these.

(a) $^-2 + ? = 8$ (b) $? + 5 = ^-10$ (c) $? + 1 = 0$ (d) $^-3 + ? = 8$

4 Copy and complete these.

(a) $100 - 110 = ?$ (b) $110 - 100 = ?$ (c) $100 - ? = ^-200$

(d) $0 - ? = ^-10$ (e) $25 - ? = ^-75$ (f) $150 - ? = ^-100$

(g) $^-20 - ? = ^-33$ (h) $? - 8 = ^-9$ (i) $? + 7 = ^-6$

5 Write down a calculation and the answer for each of these.

(a) The temperature of a metal in a laboratory is 22°C.
The metal has to be cooled by 150 degrees for an experiment.
What temperature does the metal need to be for the experiment?

(b) The freezing point of chlorine is $^-101$°C.
The boiling point is 67 degrees higher.
What is the boiling point of chlorine?

(c) The temperature in a shed was $^-11$°C at 4 a.m. and rose by
19 degrees by 4 p.m. What was the temperature at 4 p.m.?

Section C

1 In the Scholastic Skating competition, the judges give points.
If they do not like a competitor, they give negative points.

Work out the scores of each of these skaters.

(a)  (b)

(c)  (d)

2 Work out each of these additions.

(a) $^-1 + ^-2 + 4 = $ **?** (b) $^-2 + 4 + ^-2 = $ **?** (c) $^-3 + ^-3 + ^-1 = $ **?**

(d) $^-2 + 0 + 2 = $ **?** (e) $6 + ^-4 + ^-3 = $ **?** (f) $^-1 + ^-1 + 5 = $ **?**

3 Work out what **?** stands for in each of these.

(a) $^-1 + $ **?** $ = ^-4$ (b) $6 + $ **?** $ = 4$ (c) $4 + $ **?** $ + ^-1 = 0$

(d) **?** $ + 4 = 0$ (e) $5 + $ **?** $ + 2 = 1$ (f) $^-1 + ^-1 + $ **?** $ = ^-2$

4 Find the totals for each of these sets of points.

(a) | 4 | ⁻1 | ⁻2 |

(b) | 0 | ⁻1 | ⁻3 |

(c) | ⁻1 | ⁻1 | ⁻1 | ⁻1 |

(d) | 0 | ⁻5 | 5 | ⁻2 |

(e) | ⁻3 | ⁻4 | 3 | 5 |

(f) | ⁻10 | 11 | ⁻15 | 12 | ⁻9 |

5 A skater is given scores 7, 5 and $^-4$.

    (a) What is the skater's total?

    (b) After a protest, the score of $^-4$ is removed.

       What is the skater's score now?

    (c) Write a subtraction that shows the removal of the $^-4$.

6 A skater is given a total score of 10. Then a score of $^-4$ is removed.

    (a) What is her score now?

    (b) Write a subtraction to show this.

7 Write subtractions to show these.

    (a) A skater has a total of 12. Then $^-3$ is removed.

    (b) A score of $^-5$ is taken off a total of 6.

    (c) $^-6$ is taken off a total of $^-1$.

8 Work out the following subtractions.

    (a) $12 - {}^-3$ (b) $10 - {}^-8$ (c) $0 - {}^-4$

    (d) $^-3 - {}^-4$ (e) $^-1 - {}^-1$ (f) $4 - {}^-1$

9 Work out the following. Be careful!
Some are additions and some are subtractions.

    (a) $^-2 + {}^-3$ (b) $^-2 - {}^-3$ (c) $0 + {}^-3$

    (d) $0 - {}^-3$ (e) $5 + {}^-2$ (f) $^-3 - {}^-2$

    (g) $^-7 - {}^-4$ (h) $^-6 + 4$ (i) $^-4 - 10$

    (j) $4 + {}^-12$ (k) $100 - {}^-35$ (l) $^-80 - {}^-23$

10 Work out what **?** stands for in each of these.

    (a) $^-5 - {?} = 12$ (b) $2 - {?} = 10$ (c) ${?} - {}^-12 = 20$

    (d) ${?} - {}^-4 = {}^-12$ (e) $^-2 + {?} = {}^-12$ (f) $^-2 - {?} = {}^-12$

    (g) $0 + {?} = {}^-89$ (h) $^-15 - {?} = 15$ (i) ${?} + {}^-45 = {}^-50$

    (j) $^-70 - {?} = 100$ (k) ${?} - {}^-23 = {}^-45$ (l) ${?} - {}^-45 = 45$

Spot the rule

Section A

1 Copy and complete these tables.

(a)

$n \rightarrow n - 7$
$10 \rightarrow ...$
$20 \rightarrow ...$
$8 \rightarrow ...$
$33 \rightarrow ...$
$... \rightarrow 10$
$... \rightarrow 0$

(b)

$n \rightarrow 3n$
$4 \rightarrow 12$
$5 \rightarrow ...$
$8 \rightarrow ...$
$13 \rightarrow ...$
$... \rightarrow 30$
$... \rightarrow 21$

(c)

$n \rightarrow 8 - n$
$3 \rightarrow 5$
$6 \rightarrow ...$
$1 \rightarrow ...$
$\frac{1}{2} \rightarrow ...$
$... \rightarrow 4$
$... \rightarrow 8$

2 This is Adeel's rule: *number → (number divided by 2) – 1*

(a) Write his rule in a shorter way.

What happens to each of these numbers?

(b) 6   (c) 12   (d) 30   (e) 11

3 Copy and complete these tables.

(a)

$n \rightarrow 10n - 2$
$3 \rightarrow ...$
$4 \rightarrow ...$
$7 \rightarrow ...$
$8 \rightarrow ...$
$... \rightarrow 98$

(b)

$n \rightarrow \frac{n}{3}$
$15 \rightarrow ...$
$21 \rightarrow ...$
$60 \rightarrow ...$
$36 \rightarrow ...$
$... \rightarrow 9$

(c)

$n \rightarrow 30 - 2n$
$4 \rightarrow ...$
$6 \rightarrow ...$
$9 \rightarrow ...$
$11 \rightarrow ...$
$... \rightarrow 14$

4 Find the rule for each of these tables. Write each rule using $n \rightarrow ...$

(a)

$n \rightarrow ...$
$1 \rightarrow 3$
$10 \rightarrow 21$
$100 \rightarrow 201$
$5 \rightarrow 11$

(b)

$n \rightarrow ...$
$1 \rightarrow 3$
$10 \rightarrow 39$
$2 \rightarrow 7$
$5 \rightarrow 19$
$100 \rightarrow 399$

Section B

1 Copy and complete each table.
Look carefully at the rule in each table.

(a)

$n \to n^2 + 2$
3 → 11
5 → ...
8 → ...
10 → ...
2 → ...
12 → ...

(b)

$n \to n^2 + n$
1 → 2
5 → ...
10 → ...
6 → ...
9 → ...
4 → ...

(c)

$n \to n \times (n + 1)$
1 → ...
5 → ...
10 → ...
6 → ...
9 → ...
4 → ...

2 Nikki starts her game like this.

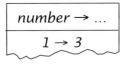

number → ...
1 → 3

(a) Which of these could her rule be?

$n \to 3n^2$		$n \to n^2 + 2$		$n \to (3n)^2$		$n \to 4n - 3$

(b) Find three more rules which might fit Nikki's game.

(c) Another line is added to Nikki's game.
Which of the rules in (a) is being used?

(d) Copy and complete the rest of the game.

number → ...
1 → 3
5 → 75
2 → ...
10 → ...
7 → ...

3 Can you spot the rule
for each of these tables?

Write the rule in the form

$$n \to \text{...}$$

if you can.

(a)

$n \to$ ...
3 → 8
5 → 24
8 → 63
10 → 99
2 → 3

(b)

$n \to$ ...
2 → 40
3 → 90
5 → 250
7 → 490
9 → 810

51

⑳ Chance

Sections D, E and F

A 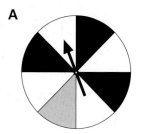 **B**   **C**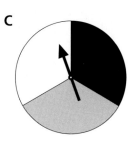

1 For each spinner, what is the probability that
   (a) white will win   (b) black will win
   (c) grey will win   (d) black will not win

2 You have decided to bet that
   (a) white will win   (b) black will win   (c) grey will win
   Which spinner would you choose in each case?

3 Write down three fractions equivalent to
   (a) $\frac{1}{4}$ (b) $\frac{3}{5}$ (c) $\frac{5}{8}$ (d) $\frac{4}{7}$

4 Simplify each of these fractions as far as possible.
   (a) $\frac{4}{8}$ (b) $\frac{8}{12}$ (c) $\frac{9}{15}$ (d) $\frac{16}{24}$ (e) $\frac{35}{60}$

5 One fraction in each set is not equivalent to the others. Which one?
   (a) $\frac{3}{6}$ $\frac{15}{30}$ $\frac{25}{55}$ $\frac{9}{18}$
   (b) $\frac{9}{15}$ $\frac{4}{6}$ $\frac{30}{45}$ $\frac{22}{33}$
   (c) $\frac{35}{50}$ $\frac{8}{10}$ $\frac{40}{50}$ $\frac{88}{110}$

6 Some of these fractions can be simplified.
   Simplify those that can as far as possible.
   (a) $\frac{24}{36}$ (b) $\frac{12}{35}$ (c) $\frac{30}{140}$ (d) $\frac{8}{54}$

7 Imagine these cards are turned over and shuffled around when you are not looking.

You choose a card at random.

What is the probability you will choose a card with

(a) the number 4   (b) the number 6   (c) a square number

(d) a multiple of 3   (e) a number greater than 25

(f) a two-digit number

8 Ann likes orange (**O**) sweets but not yellow (**Y**) ones.
She can pick a sweet at random from either bag A or B.
From which bag should she pick?
Why?

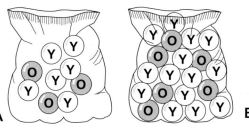

9 Rick likes blue (**B**) sweets, but not yellow (**Y**) or green (**G**) ones.
He can pick a sweet at random from bag P, Q or R.
From which bag should he pick?
Why?

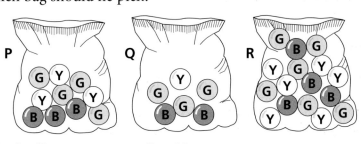

If Rick liked yellow sweets as well as blue,
from which bag should he pick?

Section G

The maximum when 3 and 5 are thrown is 5.

1 Two ordinary dice are rolled.

(a) Copy and complete this table showing the maximum of the two numbers. (If both numbers are 3, then the maximum is 3.)

(b) What is the most likely value of the maximum?

(c) What is the probability of this value?

Dice 2

	1	2	3	4	5	6
6						
5			5			
4						
3						
2						
1						

Dice 1

2 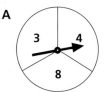 A

  B

  C

Spinners A and B are spun.
Each square in this diagram shows a possible outcome.
The shaded squares show the outcomes where A has the higher score.

What is the probability that A has the higher score?

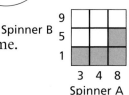

Spinner B

Spinner A

3 Spinners B and C are spun.
What is the probability that B has the higher score?

4 Spinners A and C are spun.
What is the probability that C has the higher score?

*5 Two players choose a spinner each.
(They can't both choose the same one.)
If you were one of the players, would you prefer to choose your spinner first, or last? Why?

*6 If three people play with a spinner each, what is the probability that

(a) spinner A wins   (b) spinner B wins   (c) spinner C wins

㉑ Translation

Sections A and B

1 Write down the column vector
   of each of these translations.

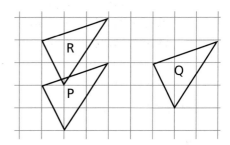

   (a) P to Q   (b) P to R

   (c) Q to R   (d) Q to P

   (e) R to P   (f) R to Q

2 This is part of an infinite pattern.

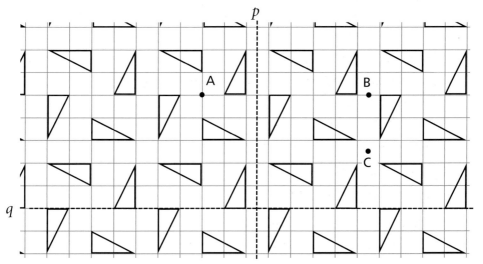

   (a) Does each of these translations move the pattern on to itself?

     (i) $\begin{bmatrix} 3 \\ 0 \end{bmatrix}$ (ii) $\begin{bmatrix} 3 \\ -5 \end{bmatrix}$ (iii) $\begin{bmatrix} 5 \\ -5 \end{bmatrix}$ (iv) $\begin{bmatrix} 10 \\ 5 \end{bmatrix}$ (v) $\begin{bmatrix} -5 \\ -10 \end{bmatrix}$

   (b) Is each of these lines a line of symmetry of the pattern?

     (i) p (ii) q

   (c) What is the order of rotation symmetry about (i) A (ii) B (iii) C

23 Number grids

Sections A and B

1 (a) Copy and complete these number grids.
(b) What is the diagonal rule for each grid?

(i)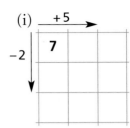

(ii) 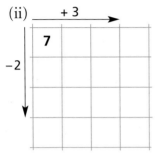   (iii) 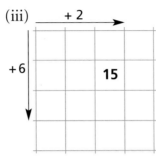   (iv)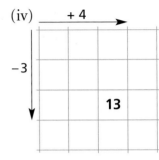

2 Find the missing rule for each of these grids.

(a) 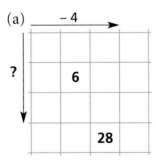   (b)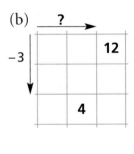

Section C

1 (a) Copy and complete each of these grids.

(b) For each grid, work out the number in the bottom right square when the number in the top left is 100.

(i) 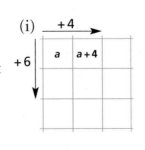   (ii)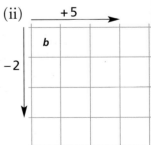

(c) For each grid, what number in the top left square would give 100 in the bottom right square?

2 Find the rules for each of these grids.

(a)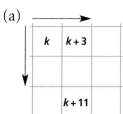

(b)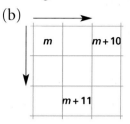

(c)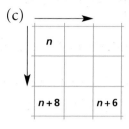

3 Write each of these in a simpler way.

(a) $t + 5 + 6$

(b) $a + 3 + 4$

(c) $q + 5 + 1$

(d) $p + 1 + 2 + 1$

(e) $x + 2 + 4 + 4$

(f) $y + 5 - 3$

(g) $s - 2 - 2$

(h) $v - 1 - 3 - 1$

(i) $b - 3 + 9$

(j) $a + 3 - 7$

(k) $f - 7 - 9$

(l) $c - 5 + 12 - 5$

(m) $d - 6 + 1 - 6$

(n) $g + 3 - 4 + 3 - 4$

(o) $h - 2 - 5 - 2 - 5$

Sections D, E and F

This chain of numbers is made using the rules '+ 2' and '+ 3'.

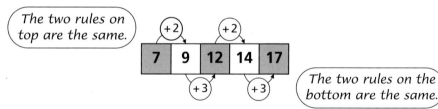

The two rules on top are the same.

The two rules on the bottom are the same.

1 Copy and complete these chains.

(a)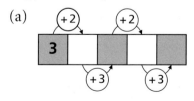

(b)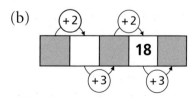

(c)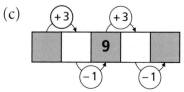

(d)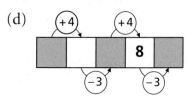

57

2 Find the missing rule in each of these.

(a)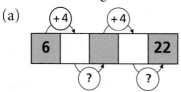

(b)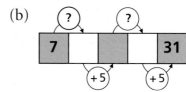

(c)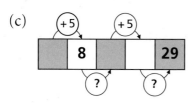

(d)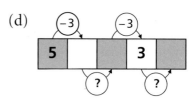

3 Find three different pairs of rules for this chain.

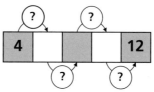

4 These chains are all made using the rules '+ 5' and '+ 2'.
For each chain, to find the ends total you add the first and last number.

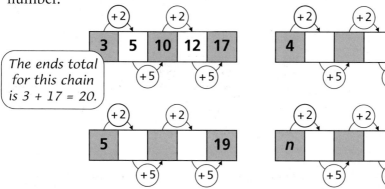

The ends total for this chain is 3 + 17 = 20.

(a) Copy and complete the chains.

(b) Copy and complete the ends total table.

(c) If the first number is 8, what is the ends total?

First number	Ends total
3	20
4	
5	
n	

5 Investigate other chains using your own pairs of rules.
Try to use algebra to explain your conclusions.

6 Find three pairs of
equivalent expressions.

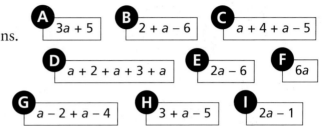

A $3a + 5$ **B** $2 + a - 6$ **C** $a + 4 + a - 5$

D $a + 2 + a + 3 + a$ **E** $2a - 6$ **F** $6a$

G $a - 2 + a - 4$ **H** $3 + a - 5$ **I** $2a - 1$

7 Write each of these in a simpler way.

(a) $p + p + 3$ (b) $y + 9 + y + y$ (c) $q + 8 + q + 2$

(d) $t + t + 5 - 2$ (e) $x + 6 + x - 4$ (f) $r + r - 2 + 8 + r$

(g) $w + w - 5 - 8$ (h) $j + j + 7 - 10$ (i) $h - 9 + h + 3$

8 These grids use the rules '+ 3' and '+ 2'.

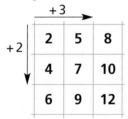

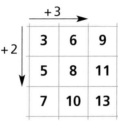

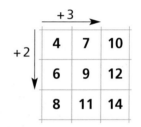

(a) You can find the grid total for each one
by adding all the numbers in the grid.
Copy and complete the grid total table.

(b) For these grids, find a rule that links the
grid total to the top left number.

(c) What would the grid total be when
the number in the top left is 50?

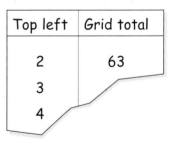

Top left	Grid total
2	63
3	
4	

9 Investigate grid totals for other sets of grids using your
own pairs of rules. Try to use algebra to explain your conclusions.

10 Simplify these expressions where possible.

(a) $3n \times 2n$ (b) $5p \times 7$ (c) $2 + 4m - 5$

(d) $12q - 2$ (e) $a \times 3a$ (f) $4s - 3 - 3s + 8$

24 Constructions

Section C

1   Draw a line *l* and mark a point A on it.
Use ruler and compasses to construct a line through A
perpendicular to *l*.

Use ruler and compasses to bisect one of the right angles.
(This is the construction for an angle of 45°.)

2   Draw a line *l* and mark a point A on it.

Draw an arc, centred at A,
cutting the line *l* at B.

Do not alter the radius.
Draw an arc, centred at B,
to cross the first arc at C.

(a) What is the size of angle CAB?

(b) Bisect angle CAB using ruler and compasses.

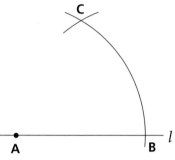

3   Draw a circle (radius about 5 to 6 cm).

Draw any three lines forming a
triangle inside the circle, like this.

Mark a point P on the circle.

Use ruler and compasses to construct
the line from P perpendicular to one
of the three lines.

Mark the point A where it cuts the line.

Do the same for each of the other two lines,
marking points B and C.

What do you notice about the points A, B and C?

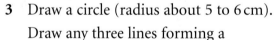

25 Comparisons 1

Sections A, B and C

1 These dot plots show the weights of some litters of puppies.
   For each one, find the median weight of the puppies.

(a) Dalmatians

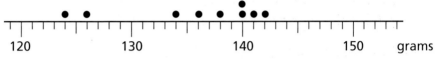

(b) Golden retrievers

(c) Labradors

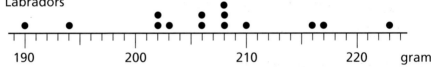

2 On graph paper, draw a number line from 110 to 150.
   (a) Draw a dot plot for the weights of these puppies.
       120 g   142 g   118 g   135 g   145 g   129 g
   (b) What is the median weight of the puppies?

3 Here are the temperatures one week in Barcelona and in Birmingham.
   Barcelona   21°C   22°C   19°C   26°C   30°C   21°C   18°C
   Birmingham   17°C   22°C   23°C   21°C   25°C   25°C   21°C
   (a) What is the median temperature in each city?
   (b) Which city has the higher median temperature that week?
   (c) What is the range of temperatures in each city?

Sections C and E

1 Here are some caterpillars, drawn full-size.
Find the median length of the caterpillars in
millimetres and the range of their lengths.

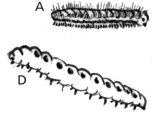

A

B    C    D

E    F

2 Find the median and range of each of these sets of data.
   (a) 73 kg, 85 kg, 102 kg, 56 kg, 88 kg, 98 kg, 75 kg
   (b) 7.6 m, 8.2 m, 6.9 m, 9 m, 6.8 m, 10.1 m, 6.8 m, 8 m
   (c) 5°C, ⁻2°C, 0°C, 3°C, ⁻5°C, 1°C, 2°C
   (d) 36.8°C, 37.2°C, 39.6°C, 39.2°C, 38.4°C, 37.7°C, 36.9°C

3 In Britain there are two types of squirrels, red and grey.
These are the weights of two samples of squirrels.

Red   278 g   297 g   303 g   282 g
       291 g   299 g   286 g   295 g

Grey   542 g   654 g   596 g   562 g
       636 g   602 g   582 g   613 g

How do the weights of the red and grey squirrels compare?

4 These are the 400 metre times (in seconds) for two runners.
How do the two runners compare?

Jo   80.5, 79.3, 81.2, 78.3, 81.7, 80.1, 79.8

Jay   82.2, 84.3, 81.2, 80.8, 76.2, 84.5, 78.0, 82.9

5 Draw diagrams, like the one on the right
to summarise the data in question 4.

8 ◄——— Range 14 ———► 22
      Median 17

Section H

1 Here are the ages of the people on a group holiday.
   Find the median age.

   22, 22, 22, 23, 23, 23, 23, 24, 24, 25, 25, 25, 26, 26, 26, 27, 28

2 The ages of another group are summarised in this table.

Age	21	22	23	24	25	26	27
Number of people	4	3	2	2	5	3	4

   (a) How many people are there in the group?

   (b) What is the median age of the group?

3 The ages of a third group are summarised in this table.

Age	21	22	23	24	25	26	27
Number of people	3	4	5	4	4	3	1

   What is the median age of the group?

4 Nina did a survey of how many TVs people had at home.
   Here is a summary of her data.

Number of TVs	0	1	2	3	4	5
Number of homes	3	13	9	4	3	1

   What is the median number of TVs?

5 This chart shows the ages
   of a group of students.

   Find the median age of
   the group.

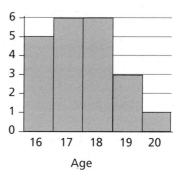

26 Further areas

Section A

1 Find the area of each of these parallelograms.

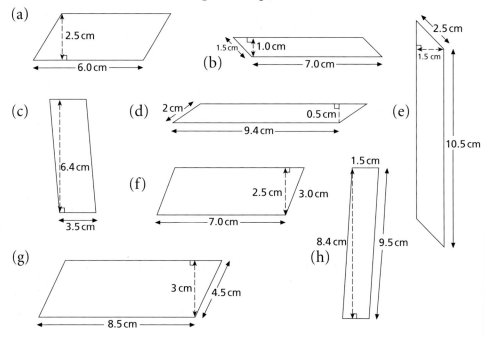

2 The area of each of these parallelograms is 36 cm².
Find the missing length in each one.

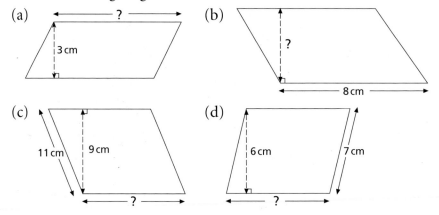

Section B

1   Put these triangles into groups so that the triangles in each group have the same area.

For each group say
  • which triangles are in it
  • what the areas of the triangles are

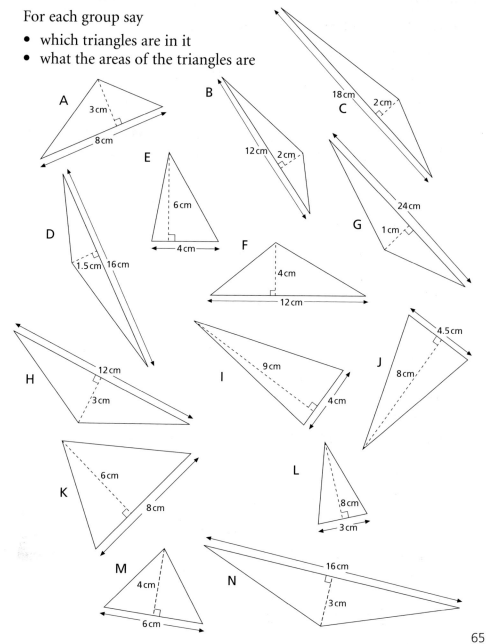

2 Find the area of each of these triangles.
They are not drawn accurately.

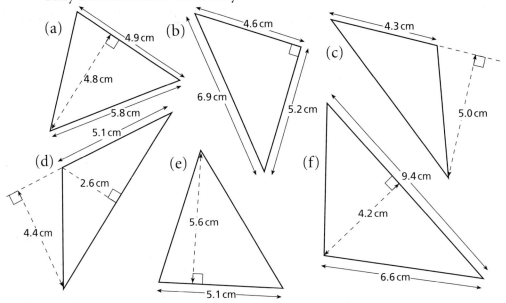

(a) 4.9 cm, 4.8 cm, 5.8 cm, 5.1 cm

(b) 4.6 cm, 6.9 cm, 5.2 cm

(c) 4.3 cm, 5.0 cm

(d) 2.6 cm, 4.4 cm

(e) 5.6 cm, 5.1 cm

(f) 9.4 cm, 4.2 cm, 6.6 cm

3 Work out the shaded areas by taking
appropriate measurements.

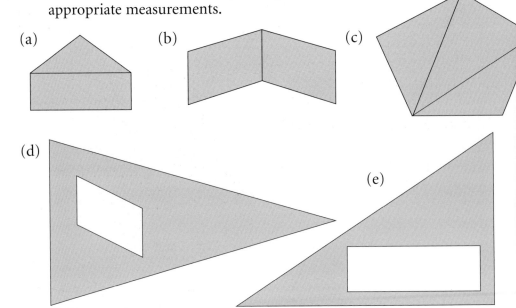

(a)

(b)

(c)

(d)

(e)

Section C

1 Put these trapeziums into groups so that the trapeziums in each group have the same area.

For each group say

- which trapeziums are in it
- what the area of each trapezium is

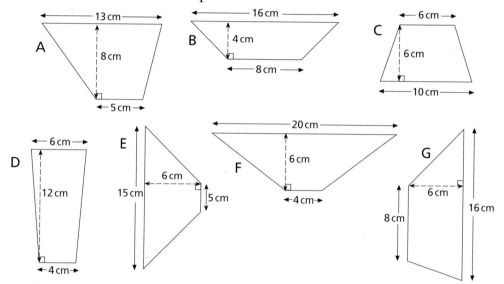

2 This diagram shows the roof of a house. It is made up of two identical triangles and two identical trapeziums.

Calculate the area of the roof.

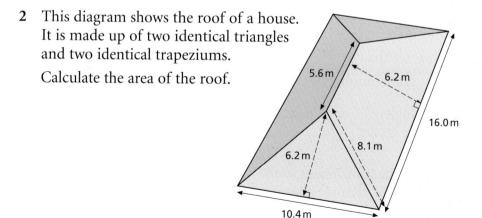

Mixed questions 3

1 Without using a calculator, find the area of each of these shapes.

(a)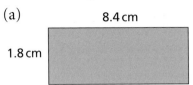

(b)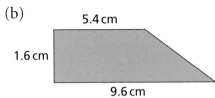

2 Work these out without using a calculator.

(a) $4 + {}^-7$ (b) $^-2 - {}^-6$ (c) $3 - {}^-4$ (d) $^-11 - 4$ (e) $^-8 - {}^-2$

3 (a) Find the rule for this table in the form
$n \rightarrow \ldots$

    (b) What is the missing number?

$n \rightarrow$ ...
$8 \rightarrow 128$
$10 \rightarrow 200$
$6 \rightarrow 72$
$7 \rightarrow$ ...

4 Steve has these cards.

He shuffles them and puts them face down.

His friend Jack picks up a card. What is the probability that
the number on Jack's card is

(a) greater than 3   (b) an odd number   (c) a prime number

(d) a square number   (e) a cube number   (f) greater than 9

5 The triangle ABC is translated
using the vector $\begin{bmatrix} -2 \\ 3 \end{bmatrix}$.

What are the coordinates of the
vertices of the triangle after it
has been translated?

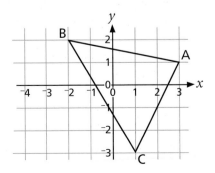

6 In this number grid, the rule across is '+ 3' and the rule down is '– 2'.

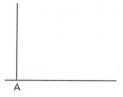

(a) Copy the grid and write expressions for the numbers in the blank squares.

(b) Find an expression for the total of all the numbers in the grid.
Write it as simply as possible.

7 In this question you may use only a ruler and compasses.

(a) Draw a line and mark a point A on it.
Construct a right angle at A.

(b) Mark a point B on your first line.
Construct a square, one of whose sides is AB.

(c) Draw the diagonals of the square and label their point of intersection C.

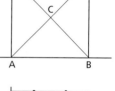

(d) Put your compasses point at A and draw an arc through C.
Mark with dots the points where the arc crosses the sides of the square.

(e) Now do the same from each other corner of the square.

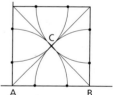

(f) Join the dots with straight line segments.
What shape have you made?

8 The number of seats sold for the 20 performances of a play were as follows:

42 45 38 38 30 27 40 31 22 18

9 12 17 21 9 14 25 14 34 37

Find the median and range of the number of seats sold.

9 Calculate the area of this field.

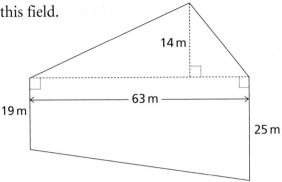

10 What fraction of this field is shaded?

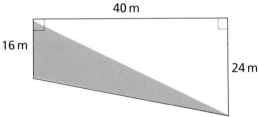

11 Pritti has a spinner like this.
The probability that the arrow lands on grey is $\frac{1}{2}$.

She replaces the circular base by a rectangular one.
Is the probability that the arrow lands on grey still $\frac{1}{2}$?
Explain the reason for your answer.

12 Given that $132 \times 47 = 6204$, write down the answer to each of these without using a calculator.

(a) 1.32×0.47 (b) 13.2×0.0047 (c) 1320×0.047

27 Inputs and outputs

Sections A and B

Copy and complete the tables.

1

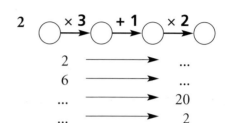

1	⟶	...
4	⟶	...
...	⟶	14
...	⟶	22

2

2	⟶	...
6	⟶	...
...	⟶	20
...	⟶	2

3 Copy and complete these arrow diagrams.
Write each of them as shorthand rules.

(a) a $\xrightarrow{-3}$ ◯ $\xrightarrow{\times 4}$ ◯

(b) a $\xrightarrow{\times 4}$ ◯ $\xrightarrow{-3}$ ◯

(c) e $\xrightarrow{\div 2}$ ◯ $\xrightarrow{-1}$ ◯

(d) e $\xrightarrow{-1}$ ◯ $\xrightarrow{\div 2}$ ◯

(e) g $\xrightarrow{\times 3}$ ◯ $\xrightarrow{-6}$ ◯

(f) h $\xrightarrow{+8}$ ◯ $\xrightarrow{\div 4}$ ◯

(g) i $\xrightarrow{-12}$ ◯ $\xrightarrow{\times 7}$ ◯

(h) s $\xrightarrow{\times 8}$ ◯ $\xrightarrow{+2}$ ◯

4 Draw arrow diagrams for these rules.

(a) $p \rightarrow 2p + 3$

(b) $m \rightarrow 2m + 6$

(c) $x \rightarrow 2(x + 3)$

(d) $b \rightarrow \frac{b}{3} + 10$

(e) $t \rightarrow \frac{t + 4}{3}$

(f) $n \rightarrow 5(n + 1)$

(g) $s \rightarrow 10(2s + 1)$

(h) $c \rightarrow 5(3 + 4c)$

Sections C and D

1 Work out the value of these.
   (a) $2(x + 1)$ when   (i) $x = 4$ (ii) $x = 10$ (iii) $x = 0$
   (b) $6p - 1$ when   (i) $p = 6$ (ii) $p = 0$ (iii) $p = 20$
   (c) $\frac{a+3}{2}$ when   (i) $a = 1$ (ii) $a = {}^{-}1$ (iii) $a = 10$

2 Which of these expressions do **not** have the value 10 when $m = 3$?

   $2m + 4$ $3m + 1$ $2(m + 2)$ $3(m + 1)$

              $4m - 2$ $10(m - 2)$ $5(m + 1)$

3 Work out the value of each of these when $x = 0$
   (a) $4(x + 1)$ (b) $4x + 1$ (c) $6x - 5$
   (d) $\frac{x+7}{2}$ (e) $3(10 + x)$ (f) $\frac{x}{2} - 4$

4 Find what you have to replace **?** by, so that whatever the input,
   the two outputs are the same.

72

Sections E and F

1 Copy and complete these, filling in the missing numbers.

(a) $2(x + 3) = 2x + \heartsuit$

(b) $\blacktriangle(x + 4) = \blacktriangle x + 16$

(c) $5x + 10 = \bullet(x + \blacksquare)$

(d) $\frac{x - \blacktriangledown}{2} = \frac{x}{\blacklozenge} - 4$

(e) $\frac{x + 12}{\bullet} = \frac{x}{2} + \text{✳}$

(f) $\text{✳}(x + 6) = \text{✳}x + 24$

2 Find an equivalent expression for each of these.

(a) $2(a + 3)$

(b) $5(x - 1)$

(c) $\frac{p + 8}{4}$

(d) $10(p + 4)$

(e) $4(s + 2\frac{1}{2})$

(f) $100(c - 1)$

(g) $\frac{y - 3}{2}$

(h) $30(m - 0.2)$

(i) $4(2a - 1)$

(j) $\frac{4j + 2}{2}$

(k) $\frac{8k - 24}{4}$

(l) $5(8a - 2)$

3 With each puzzle, describe what happens for different starting numbers and explain using algebra.

(a) Think of a number.
Add on 3.
Multiply it by 2.
Subtract 2.
Divide by 2.
Subtract your first number.
I can tell you your answer.

(b) Think of a number.
Multiply it by 5.
Add on 10.
Divide by 5.
Double it.
Subtract 4.
What is your answer?

(c) Think of a number.
Subtract 1.
Multiply by 3.
Add 6.
Divide by 3.
Subtract 1.
What is your answer?

(d) Think of a number.
Multiply by 10.
Subtract 5.
Divide by 5.
Multiply by 3.
Add 3.
What is your answer?

28 Decimals 2

Section A

Do these without a calculator.

1 (a) 0.52×0.1 (b) $0.52 \div 0.1$ (c) 6.34×0.01 (d) $6.34 \div 0.01$

2 What number is missing in each of these?

   (a) $3.47 \div \, ? = 0.0347$ (b) $3.47 \times \, ? = 0.0347$ (c) $0.682 \times \, ? = 682$

   (d) $68.2 \div \, ? = 6820$ (e) $5.03 \div \, ? = 50.3$ (f) $? \times 90.4 = 0.904$

Section B

1 Work these out without a calculator.

   (a) 0.30×50 (b) 30×50 (c) 0.03×500 (d) 300×0.5

2 Work these out without a calculator.

   (a) 7×400 (b) 0.08×200 (c) 900×400

   (d) 0.1×6000 (e) 0.4×0.5 (f) 0.06×3000

3 Here is a set of numbers:

   300   30   3   0.3   0.03
       400   40   4   0.4   0.04

   From this set, find as many pairs as possible whose product is

   (a) 120   (b) 90   (c) 1.2   (d) 16   (e) 0.12

Sections C and D

1 Round these to one significant figure.

   (a) 0.471   (b) 7401   (c) 21.93   (d) 54 431

   (e) 9.48   (f) 0.744   (g) 0.018 92   (h) 0.000 847

2 Estimate these by rounding the numbers to 1 s.f.
Show the numbers you use to get your estimate.
The first is done as an example.

(a) 42 × 79   *Estimate: 40 x 80 = 3200*

(b) 310 × 47   (c) 592 × 320   (d) 5482 × 376

(e) 47.2 × 9.8   (f) 0.3129 × 0.408   (g) 7.721 × 85.6

(h) 5725 × 0.82   (i) 409 × 0.0081   (j) 0.026 × 27.381

3 1 gallon is approximately equal to 4.55 litres.
A tank holds 3120 gallons of diesel.

Approximately how many litres is this?

4 About how much would 37 litres
of unleaded petrol cost?

PETROL
prices per litre
Unleaded   82.1p
4 star
          87.5p

Section E

Do these without a calculator.

1 (a) 23.1 × 0.7   (b) 0.3 × 0.37   (c) 450 × 0.4   (d) 4.56 × 0.005

2 You are told that 7 × 68 = 476.
Write down the answer to each of these.

(a) 0.7 × 6.8   (b) 70 × 0.68   (c) 0.007 × 6.8   (d) 0.07 × 6800

Sections F and G

1 Work these out.

(a) $\dfrac{2.8}{0.4}$ (b) $\dfrac{0.72}{0.09}$ (c) $\dfrac{3.6}{0.04}$ (d) $\dfrac{60}{0.02}$ (e) $\dfrac{270}{0.9}$

2 Work these out.

(a) $\dfrac{1.44}{0.6}$ (b) $\dfrac{384}{0.08}$ (c) $\dfrac{10.36}{700}$ (d) $\dfrac{51.2}{40}$ (e) $\dfrac{150}{0.06}$

Section H

1 Round each of these numbers to 2 s.f.
   (a) 48 120   (b) 0.042 124   (c) 9.082   (d) 0.003 713

2 Round each of these numbers to 3 s.f.
   (a) 871.36   (b) 0.041 856   (c) 27.835   (d) 310.275

3 (a) Round 0.004 8146 to 3 s.f.   (b) Round 9.008 315 to 2 s.f.
   (c) Round 4 305 609 to 4 s.f.   (d) Round 420.573 to 3 s.f.

Section I

1 (a) Round 67 810 to the nearest hundred. (b) Round 67 810 to 2 s.f.
   (c) Round 5.4367 to one decimal place.   (d) Round 5.4367 to 1 s.f.

2 (a) Round 0.040 32 to 2 d.p.   (b) Round 0.040 32 to 2 s.f.
   (c) Round 8712.48 to the nearest ten.   (d) Round 8712.48 to 1 d.p.

*3 The number in this headline has been rounded to the nearest hundred.

> **Singer attracts 6700 fans**
> Star performer Bianca Rossa delighted the hundreds of fans who flocked to hear

   (a) Which of these could have been the actual number of fans?
       6500   6683   6772   6641   6731   6702
   (b) What is the smallest actual number that would fit the headline?
   (c) What is the largest number that would fit the headline?

*4 The number in this headline has been rounded to the nearest thousand.

> **Student earns £28 000 in summer holidays**
> Computer science student Nadia Picozzi worked for local firm Update during her

   (a) Which of these could have been the actual amount Nadia earned?
       £29 000   £27 800   £26 950   £28 640   £28 428   £27 462
   (b) What is the smallest actual amount that would fit the headline?
   (c) What is the largest amount that would fit the headline?

30 Parallel lines

Section A

1 (a) Draw two parallel lines 4 cm apart.

   (b) Draw another pair 4 cm apart, crossing the first pair.

   (c) Draw these diagonals. Measure angles and lengths and write what you find.

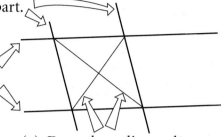

2 Jack is at point J on an orienteering challenge.

   He runs parallel to the wall ZY until he reaches the river XY.

   What are the coordinates of the point he reaches?

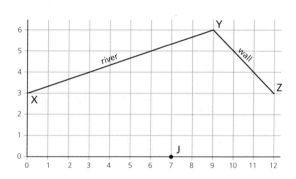

3 P, Q and R are buoys marking the site of a ship wreck.
   Harry is searching for sunken treasure.
   He has been given these directions:

   Draw a line joining P to Q.
   Draw a line joining Q to R.
   Draw a line through A parallel to PQ.
   Draw a line through B parallel to QR.
   The cargo hold is directly below
   where these two lines meet.

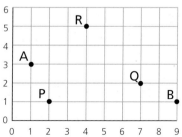

   Copy the diagram on to squared paper.
   Use the directions to find the coordinates of the cargo hold.

Sections C and D

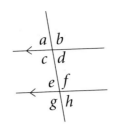

1

| corresponding angles |
| alternate angles |
| vertically opposite angles |
| supplementary angles |

Copy and complete each sentence with the correct phrase.

Angles *a* and *d* are ....　Angles *e* and *a* are ....

Angles *c* and *f* are ....　Angles *f* and *d* are ....

Angles *h* and *d* are ....　Angles *f* and *e* are ....

Angles *f* and *g* are ....　Angles *b* and *f* are ....

2 Work out the angles marked with letters.
Explain your results.

(a) 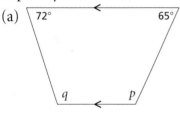 (b)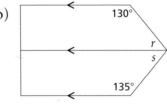

(c) 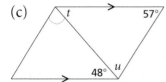 (d)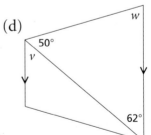

3 Work out the angles marked with letters.

(a) 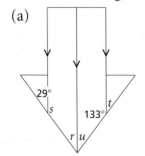 (b)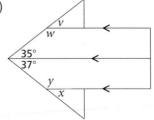

4 Work out the angles marked with a letter.
If you need to, copy the sketch and add extra lines and angles.

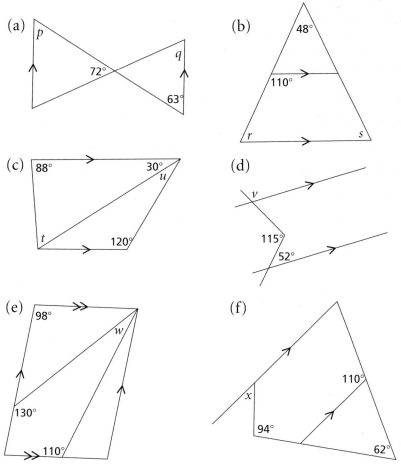

(a)

(b)

(c)

(d)

(e)

(f)

5 Work out each angle marked with a **?**.
Give reasons.

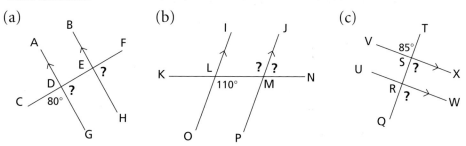

(a)

(b)

(c)

③① Percentage

Section A

1 This diagram shows the proportions of protein, fat and carbohydrate in two chocolate bars.

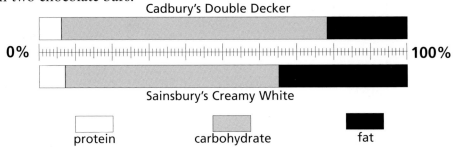

What are the percentages of protein, fat and carbohydrate in each bar?

2 These diagrams show the proportions of protein, carbohydrate, fat and fibre in two cereals.

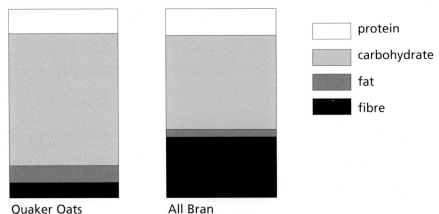

Which of the percentages on the right is nearest to

(a) the percentage of fibre in All Bran

(b) the percentage of protein in Quaker Oats

(c) the percentage of carbohydrate in Quaker Oats

(d) the percentage of carbohydrate in All Bran

| 10% |
| 30% |
| 50% |
| 70% |
| 90% |

Section B

Do not use a calculator for this section.

1 Work out these in your head.
    (a) 50% of £20   (b) 50% of £17   (c) 50% of £90

2 Work out these in your head.
    (a) 25% of £60   (b) 25% of £52   (c) 25% of £50

3 Work out these in your head.
    (a) 10% of 70 kg   (b) 10% of £75   (c) 10% of £73

4 Do these in your head. Just write the answer.
    (a) 1% of £5   (b) 3% of £5   (c) 97% of £5
    (d) 1% of £90   (e) 5% of £90

5 (a) How do you work out 10% of a number in your head?
    (b) How do you work out 5% of a number in your head?
    (c) How do you work out 15% of a number in your head?

6 In your head, work these out.
    (a) 15% of £10   (b) 15% of £40   (c) 15% of £90

7 Find the odd one out in each block.

(a)
50% of £6
3% of £10
25% of £12
10% of £30

(b)
10% of £50
100% of £5
5% of £100
25% of £20
75% of £8

(c)
25% of £18
10% of £45
5% of £80
9% of £50

Section C

1 What decimal is equivalent to

   (a) 68%   (b) 41%   (c) 80%   (d) 8%

   (e) 9%   (f) 90%   (g) 54.5%   (h) 30.5%

2 What percentage is equivalent to

   (a) 0.65   (b) 0.6   (c) 0.06   (d) 0.065

   (e) 0.02   (f) 0.22   (g) 0.2   (h) 0.202

3 Copy and complete this table.

Fraction		Decimal		Percentage
$\frac{58}{100}$	=		=	
	=	0.32	=	
$\frac{9}{100}$	=		=	
	=		=	80%
	=	0.05	=	

4 Put these in order, starting with the smallest.

   (a) $\frac{8}{100}$ $\frac{81}{100}$ 0.09   7%   0.8   0.1

   (b) 20% $\frac{1}{2}$ 0.02   0.1   12%   0.7

   (c) 75% $\frac{8}{100}$ $\frac{3}{10}$ 0.07   40%   0.3

Section D

1 Match an answer with each calculation, and write an answer for the extra calculation.

Calculation	Answer
28% of 4	0.64
47% of 220	6.643
91% of 7.3	1.12
26% of 82	103.4
8% of 8	

2 Find the odd one out.

   A 20% of £50   **B** 30% of £20   **C** 75% of £8

3 Find the odd one out.

   A 64% of 5 kg   **B** 44% of 7.5 kg   **C** 60% of 5.5 kg

4 A car is normally priced at £7995. In a sale, 15% is taken off the price.

   (a) How much is taken off?

   (b) How much does the car cost in the sale?

5 The Southern Stone Building Society pays 5% interest per year on accounts that have less than £10 000, and 6% on other accounts. How much interest will the following earn in a year?

(a) Winston, who has £8210   (b) Julie, who has £605 100

(c) Hadley, who has £47 600

Sections E and F

1 Put these fractions in order of size, smallest first. $\frac{6}{11}$ $\frac{11}{19}$ $\frac{13}{27}$

2 13 out of 17 apples are rotten.
What percentage (to the nearest 1%) are rotten?

3 In a school of 672 pupils, 83 are absent during a flu epidemic.
What percentage (to the nearest 1%) is absent?

4 A piece of fruit weighed 67.8 g when it was picked.
After heating to remove water it weighed 21.1 g.

(a) What percentage of the fruit was left after heating?

(b) What percentage of the unheated fruit was water?

5 Find the odd one out by changing each to a percentage.

   A 42 out of 168   **B** 35.5 out of 144   **C** 67.25 out of 269

6 Find the odd one out.

   A 2.22 out of 3.7   **B** 2.24 out of 4   **C** 2.16 out of 3.6

7 In 1994 the population of the UK was 58.4 million.
48.7 million lived in England, 5.1 million in Scotland,
2.9 million in Wales and the rest in Northern Ireland.

(a) What percentage of the UK population lived in Scotland?

(b) What percentage lived in England and Wales together?

(c) What percentage lived in Northern Ireland?

Sections G and H

1 Here is the breakdown of samples of two breakfast cereals.

	Protein	Carbohydrate	Fat	Fibre
Quaker Oats	11.0 g	62.0 g	8.0 g	7.0 g
All Bran	13 g	46 g	3.5 g	29 g

(a) Draw a pie chart to illustrate the data for Quaker Oats.

(b) Draw a pie chart to illustrate the data for All Bran.

(c) How do the charts compare?
   Write about any similarities or differences.

2 Here is a table of the energy consumed in the UK
   (in equivalent million tonnes of oil).

	Coal	Petroleum	Natural gas	Nuclear
1982	68.0	71.0	45.2	11.9
1995	49.8	76.2	70.0	21.4

(a) Draw two pie charts to illustrate the data.

(b) How do the charts compare?
   Write about any similarities or differences.

3 Peter bought some postcards at a stamp and postcard fair.
   The seller rounded down the price from £2.30 to £2.

(a) How much discount did he get?

(b) Calculate what percentage the discount is of £2.30.

4 Copy and complete these tables.

(a)

of	5	82	
10%	0.5		
20%		10	
	3.5		

(b)

of	30	55	
30%			6
80%			
		11	

32 Think of a number

Section A

1 Solve these puzzles by using arrow diagrams.

(a)
> I think of a number.
> - I subtract 7.
> - I multiply by 7.4.
>
> The result is 185.
> What number did I think of?

(b)
> I think of a number.
> - I multiply by 0.5.
> - I add 1.5.
>
> The result is 6.
> What number did I think of?

(c)
> I think of a number.
> - I add 5.
> - I divide by 0.3.
> - I subtract 17.
>
> The result is 9.
> What number did I think of?

(d)
> I think of a number.
> - I divide by 6.
> - I subtract 1.4.
> - I multiply by 0.2.
>
> The result is 8.
> What number did I think of?

2 The result for this number puzzle is missing.

(a) Choose a number for the result.
Solve the number puzzle for your result.

(b) Solve the number puzzle for some different results.

(c) What do you notice?
Try to explain this.

> I think of a number.
> - I add 1.
> - I multiply by 4.
> - I add 6.
> - I divide by 2.
> - I subtract 5.
>
> The result is
> What num

Section B

1 Write an equation for this number puzzle.
Use n to stand for the number.

> I think of a number.
> - I multiply by 54.
>
> The result is 378.
> What number did I think of?

2 Write an equation for each of these number puzzles.
Use n to stand for the number each time.

(a)
> I think of a number.
> - I multiply by 7.
> - I add 3.
>
> The result is 206.
> What number did I think of?

(b)
> I think of a number.
> - I subtract 13.
> - I divide by 4.
>
> The result is 6.1.
> What number did I think of?

3 Write an equation for each arrow diagram.

(a)

(b)

(c)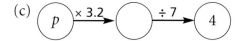

(d)

(e)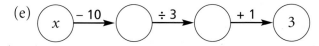

Section C

1 Solve these equations by using arrow diagrams.

(a) $11(w + 7) = 198$ (b) $7n - 5 = 51$ (c) $12p + 3 = 375$

(d) $\frac{x}{3} - 2 = 3.1$ (e) $\frac{a + 3}{4} = 20$ (f) $\frac{y - 3}{8} = 4.5$

(g) $17(p - 5) = 306$ (h) $\frac{h}{6} + 5 = 7.7$ (i) $\frac{t + 4}{13} = 12$

2 Solve these equations.

(a) $7x - 4.7 = 31$ (b) $6a + 3.2 = 29$ (c) $0.2y - 4 = 6$

(d) $\frac{m}{7} + 4.4 = 5$ (e) $\frac{w - 4.9}{5.2} = 2$ (f) $0.4(h - 2) = 3.8$

(g) $32(k + 1.5) = 480$ (h) $\frac{m + 8.1}{2.5} = 90$ (i) $\frac{n}{2.9} - 11 = 5$

3 Make up three different equations that have $x = 4$ as a solution.

4 Make up two different equations that have $p = 2.5$ as a solution.

5 Make up two different equations that have $n = 7.1$ as a solution.

6 Solve these equations.

(a) $5(x - 7) - 13 = 32$

(b) $2.5(d + 16) - 69 = 6$

(c) $\dfrac{y - 6}{3.4} + 1.5 = 5$

(d) $\dfrac{6m}{2.1} - 4 = 16$

(e) $\dfrac{b + 4.3}{0.6} - 29 = 6$

(f) $\dfrac{7n - 16}{4} + 34 = 58$

*7 The numbers p, q, r and s are connected by the formula
$$s = pq + r$$
Work out
(a) the value of s when $p = 4.5$, $q = 1.2$ and $r = 7.5$
(b) the value of r when $s = 10.5$, $p = 1.5$ and $q = 6$
(c) the value of q when $s = 16.5$, $p = 3.5$ and $r = 8.1$
(d) the value of p when $s = 8$, $q = 0.4$ and $r = 4.6$

*8 The numbers w, x, y and z are connected by the formula
$$w = \frac{x}{y} - z$$
Work out the value of x when $w = 1.4$, $y = 5$ and $z = 0.2$.

33 Quadrilaterals

Section B

1 For this question, work on square dotty paper if you like.
   Do drawings to show how
   (a) a square can be split into two trapeziums
   (b) a rhombus can be split into two parallelograms
   (c) a kite can be split into a rhombus and an arrowhead
   (d) a rectangle can be split into two trapeziums and a parallelogram
   (e) a square can be split into two arrowheads and a rhombus

Section C

1 Work out the angles marked with letters.

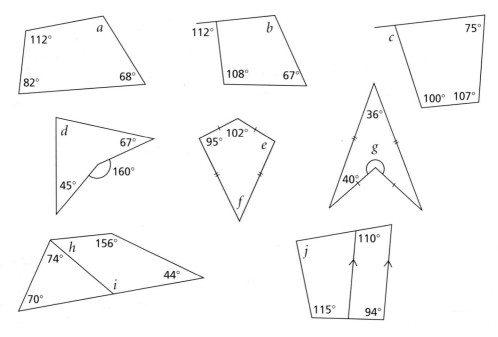

2 Work out the angles marked with letters.

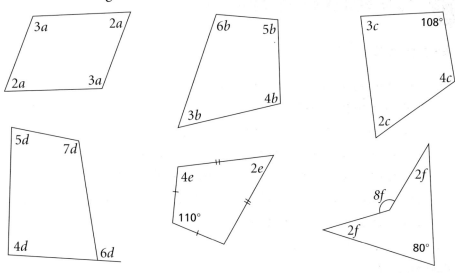

Section D

1 Do accurate drawings of the quadrilaterals sketched here.

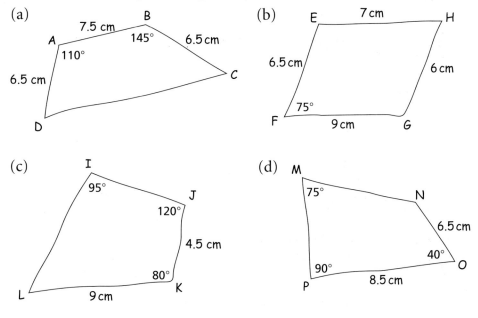

34 Negative numbers 2

Sections A and B

1. Work these out.

   (a) $^-9 + {}^-4$ (b) $^-8 - {}^-2$ (c) $3 - {}^-6$ (d) $^-2 - {}^-7$

2. Given that $x = {}^-3$ and $y = {}^-5$, find the value of

   (a) $2x + 1$ (b) $10 - y$ (c) $4 - 3x$ (d) $4y + 5$ (e) $2x - 3y$

3. Given that $a = 4$ and $b = {}^-8$, find the value of

   (a) $^-12 - 3a$ (b) $3 - 7a$ (c) $11 - 2b$ (d) $3b + 5$ (e) $5a - 3b$

4. I think of a number, square it and subtract 7. The result is 2.
   What could my number be?

5. I think of a number, square it and multiply by 4. The result is 100.
   What could my number be?

Sections C and D

1. Given that $r = {}^-4$ and $s = {}^-8$, find the value of

   (a) $\frac{r}{2} + 1$ (b) $5 - \frac{r}{2}$ (c) $^-2 + \frac{s}{4}$ (d) $10 - \frac{s}{2}$ (e) $\frac{s}{2} + \frac{r}{4}$

2. Given that $p = {}^-2$ and $q = {}^-3$, find the value of

   (a) $\frac{10}{p} - 1$ (b) $6 + \frac{12}{q}$ (c) $13 - \frac{8}{p}$ (d) $7 - \frac{21}{q}$ (e) $\frac{6}{p} - \frac{6}{q}$

3. What is the input of this arrow
   diagram if the output is

   (a) 1   (b) 21   (c) $^-19$

   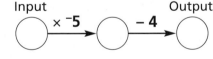

   Input $\times\,^-5$ $-\,4$ Output

4. Solve these 'think of a number' problems.

   (a) I think of a number, divide it by $^-3$ and subtract 6.
   The result is $^-8$.

   (b) I think of a number, subtract 4 and multiply by $^-4$.
   The result is 12.

35 Comparisons 2

Section A

1   Kathy has 6 goes at skittles. Her scores are 4, 3, 0, 6, 2, 6.
    Then Mark has 10 goes. His scores are 3, 1, 7, 5, 2, 4, 2, 7, 1, 2.

   (a) Who did better, Kathy or Mark?
       Give a reason for your answer.
   (b) If Mark had stopped after 4 goes, who would have done better?
       Give a reason.

2   The pupils in a class get these amounts of pocket money each week.

Girls	£3.90 £4.80 £4.00 £3.90 £3.40
	£3.70 £4.60 £4.00 £4.00 £3.70
Boys	£3.50 £3.50 £5.20 £3.70 £4.00
	£4.00 £4.00 £3.70

   (a) What is the mean amount of pocket money for the girls?
   (b) What is the mean amount for the boys?

3   What is the mean number of letters in the words in this question?

4   What is the mean value of the different types of ordinary
    British coins?

5   (a) Find three odd numbers that have a mean of 7.
    (b) Why is it not possible to find three even numbers that
        have a mean of 7?

6   Find five numbers that have a mean of 9.4.

Section B

1   Three people in a family each have 28 teeth.
The other person in the family has 26 teeth.
What is the mean number of teeth per person in the family?

2   Steve records how many people there are in cars passing his school.

Number of occupants	Number of cars
1	50
2	25
3	20
4	3
5	2

What is the mean number of people in a car?

3   A zoo has a family of smooth snakes, which are very rare in Britain.
Since 1975, every time a female snake has laid eggs,
the zoo has recorded the number of eggs.

Number of eggs	Frequency
4	5
5	1
6	4
7	1
8	9
9	5
10	10
11	2
12	8
13	1
14	4

What is the mean number of eggs laid?

4   These are the recorded weights in grams of 25 frogs
    that a naturalist has caught.

            190 150 280 150 130 150 300 210 150 320
            170 170 160 260 180 290 290 240 270 140
            140 310 320 200 200

(a) Calculate the mean weight of the frogs.

(b) Draw a scale like this on graph paper.
    Mark dots for all the frogs.

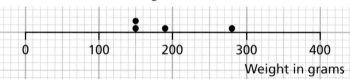

The naturalist knows that the frogs are a mixture of marsh frogs
and edible frogs. The two kinds look similar, but marsh frogs are
heavier than edible frogs.

(c) From your dot plot, how many do you think are marsh frogs?

(d) Work out the mean weight of those you think are marsh frogs.

(e) Work out the mean weight of those you think are edible frogs.

Section E

1   In class of 30 pupils the mean weight of the 10 boys is 47.2 kg and
    the mean weight of the 20 girls is 42.4 kg.

    What is the mean weight of a pupil in the class?

2   The heights of the members of a male rowing crew are

            1.74 m 1.89 m 1.88 m 2.07 m 2.04 m 1.91 m 1.98 m 1.92 m

(a) Calculate their mean height.

(b) The height of the cox is 1.46 m.
    Without calculating, make an estimate of the mean height
    of the crew if he is included in it.

(c) Now calculate the mean height with him included.

3   These are St Mary's netball results for the first 10 games of the season.

St Mary's	7	6	1	3	9	11	5	8	2	14
Opposing team	2	7	2	5	10	5	13	10	3	4

(a) What is the mean score for St Mary's?

(b) What is the mean score for the opposing teams?

(c) Did St Mary's win most of the games?
Do the answers to (a) and (b) allow you to predict this?

(d) The first game was won by a margin of 5 goals.
The second was won by a margin of 1 goal.
Work out the mean goal margin for all these games.
Do the answers to (a) and (b) allow you to predict this?

4   In a committee of six people, one member leaves and
is replaced by a new member.
As a result the mean age of the committee goes down from 42 to 39.

What does this tell you about the ages of the member who left and
the one who joined?

*5   Find a set of seven different positive whole numbers whose mean is 8,
median is 5 and range is 13.

How many different sets can you find?

Mixed questions 4

1 Copy and complete each of these.

(a) $3(p + 5) = \ldots p + \ldots$

(b) $4q - 12 = \ldots(q - \ldots)$

(c) $\dfrac{20r - 8}{4} = \ldots r - \ldots$

(d) $\dfrac{s + 14}{2} = \ldots s + \ldots$

2 You are told that $245 \times 106 = 25\,970$.
Without using a calculator, write down the answer to each of these.

(a) $2597 \div 10.6$

(b) 24.5×0.106

(c) 0.245×0.106

(d) $2.597 \div 0.245$

(e) $259.7 \div 1060$

(f) $2597 \div 24\,500$

3 Calculate the angle marked x.
Give a reason for each step of your working.

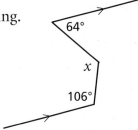

4 Without using a calculator, work these out.

(a) 25% of £13

(b) 20% of £48

(c) 15% of £70

(d) 30% of £28

(e) 95% of £18

(f) 12.5% of £40

5 Which of the types of quadrilateral listed below

(a) may have just one line of reflection symmetry

(b) cannot have just one line of reflection symmetry

Draw diagrams, where appropriate, to illustrate your answers.

trapezium   rhombus   parallelogram

rectangle   kite   square

6 (a) I think of a number, multiply it by ⁻2, subtract ⁻6
   and divide by ⁻3. The result is ⁻8.

   What number did I think of?

(b) I think of a number, add ⁻10, multiply by 4, subtract ⁻8
   and divide by ⁻4. The result is ⁻4.

   What number did I think of?

7 In a football team, the mean weight of the five heaviest players
   is 85.2 kg. The mean weight of the six remaining players is 74.6 kg.

   Calculate the mean weight of the team, to the nearest 0.1 kg.

8 The line AE shows a path across a field ABCD.
   The path splits the field into two parts of equal area.
   Calculate the distance BE.

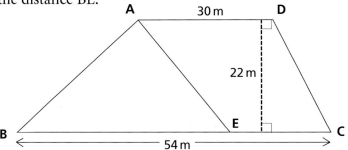

9 Solve each of these equations.

(a) $3(x - 7) = 51$

(b) $\frac{4x + 5}{9} = 3$

(c) $\frac{x}{2} - 23 = 41$

(d) $3x - 17 = {}^-2$

(e) $5x + 18 = 3$

(f) $\frac{4x - 13}{5} = {}^-9$

10 In a club, one member aged 34 leaves and is replaced by a new
   member aged 64.
   As a result, the mean age of the club goes up by 2 years.

   How many members are there in the club?

36 Know your calculator

Section A

1 Work these out without a calculator.

    (a) $5 + 14 \div 2$ (b) $7 \times 8 - 6$ (c) $15 + 4 \times 3$

    (d) $20 - 6 \times 3$ (e) $30 \div 3 + 2$ (f) $15 + 12 \div 4$

    (g) $9 \times 4 \div 3$ (h) $17 - 2 \times 3$ (i) $23 + 18 \div 3$

2 Find the missing number in each of these calculations.

    (a) $17 + 12 \div \blacksquare = 20$ (b) $8 + 3 \times \blacksquare = 17$ (c) $5 + 2 \times \blacksquare = 17$

    (d) $12 \div \blacksquare + 1 = 3$ (e) $14 + \blacksquare \div 3 = 18$ (f) $21 + \blacksquare \times 3 = 36$

    (g) $\blacksquare + 15 \div 3 = 12$ (h) $\blacksquare \div 3 - 2 = 9$ (i) $\blacksquare \times 9 - 4 = 23$

3 You can replace each diamond in the expression below
with $+, -, \times$ or $\div$.

You cannot change the order of numbers, or use brackets.

$$\boxed{36 \blacklozenge 9 \blacklozenge 3}$$

Replace each diamond with a symbol to make an expression
with the value

    (a) 12   (b) 33   (c) 9   (d) 108

4 In a game there are three number cards … $\boxed{4}$ $\boxed{8}$ $\boxed{16}$

    … and four operation cards $\boxed{+}$ $\boxed{-}$ $\boxed{\times}$ $\boxed{\div}$.

Each time you must use all the number cards and only two
operation cards, for example $\boxed{16}$ $\boxed{\times}$ $\boxed{4}$ $\boxed{-}$ $\boxed{8}$

Show how you could use the cards to make expressions
with these values.

    (a) 18   (b) 48   (c) 12   (d) 2

Sections B and C

1 Write these expressions, adding brackets where necessary, to make the result 36 each time.

(a) $3 \times 3 \times 4$ (b) $4 \times 5 + 4$ (c) $4 + 4 \times 8$

(d) $20 - 2 \times 2$ (e) $24 + 3 \times 4$ (f) $4 \times 12 - 3$

2 Put these expressions into groups so that those in each group have the same value.

A $9 + 3 \times 4$ **B** $8 \times 3 \div 2$ **C** $20 - 3 \times 5$ **D** $36 \div (14 \div 7)$

E $15 + 18 \div 6$ **F** $30 - 3 \times 3$ **G** $35 \div (8 - 1)$ **H** $48 \div (6 - 2)$

3 Which of these expressions do not need brackets?

A $12 + (4 - 2)$ **B** $12 + (4 \times 2)$ **C** $12 \div (4 + 2)$

D $12 + (4 \div 2)$ **E** $(12 \times 4) + 2$ **F** $12 - (4 - 2)$

4 Find four matching pairs of expressions.

A $24 - \dfrac{6}{3}$ **B** $(24 - 6) \div 3$ **C** $\dfrac{24}{6} - 3$ **D** $\dfrac{24}{6 - 3}$

E $24 \div 6 - 3$ **F** $24 \div (6 - 3)$ **G** $24 - (6 \div 3)$ **H** $\dfrac{24 - 6}{3}$

5 Work these out without a calculator.

(a) $\dfrac{20}{3 + 2}$ (b) $8 + \dfrac{12}{3}$ (c) $\dfrac{18 - 3}{2}$

(d) $\dfrac{30}{5} - 5$ (e) $\dfrac{48}{3 \times 4}$ (f) $12 - \dfrac{21}{3}$

(g) $\dfrac{20 - 2 \times 4}{4}$ (h) $\dfrac{36}{7 - 3} - 5$

Section D

1 Find the value of each of these.

(a) $\dfrac{24.7}{6.2 - 2.4}$

(b) $31.8 - \dfrac{19.5}{2.6}$

(c) $\dfrac{4 \times 10.2}{8 \times 0.6}$

2 Find the value of each of these.

(a) $\dfrac{15 - 7.8}{1.09 + 0.35}$

(b) $\dfrac{2.4 \times 5.2}{5 - 1.8}$

(c) $\dfrac{(7.5 + 3.7) \times 1.2}{0.3}$

(d) $5 \times \dfrac{28.8}{4.5} - 2.4$

(e) $\dfrac{(8.7 - 2.3) \times 1.5}{5.1 - 4.8}$

(f) $\dfrac{3.8 \times 8.4}{12 \times 0.4}$

Section E

1 Without using a calculator, evaluate these.

(a) $30 - 5^2$

(b) 4×3^2

(c) $12 + 3 \times 3^2$

(d) $3 \times 4^2 - 8$

(e) $(5 \times 2)^2 - 6$

(f) $\dfrac{4^2}{2}$

(g) $\dfrac{36}{3^2}$

(h) $\dfrac{6^2}{2^2}$

2 Using only the keys $\boxed{(}\ \boxed{)}\ \boxed{9}\ \boxed{4}\ \boxed{+}\ \boxed{-}\ \boxed{\div}\ \boxed{\times}\ \boxed{x^2}$
write down a set of key presses to evaluate these.

(a) 9×4^2

(b) $\dfrac{9 - 4^2}{4}$

(c) $\dfrac{4 + 9^2}{4^2}$

(d) $\dfrac{9}{9 - 4^2}$

3 Evaluate these.

(a) 0.3×6^2

(b) $(2.3 + 4.2)^2$

(c) $\dfrac{6.3 - 0.5^2}{1.21}$

(d) $\dfrac{3.5 \times 4^2}{32}$

(e) $\dfrac{(2.5 \times 4.2)^2}{30 - 4.8}$

(f) $10 - \dfrac{2.4^2}{4}$

(g) $\dfrac{7.2 + 2.1^2}{0.5 \times 3.87}$

(h) $\dfrac{(10 - 2.8^2) \times 4}{1.92}$

(i) $\dfrac{2.5 + 4.7 \times 4^2}{7^2 + 6.5}$

(j) $3 \times (2.5^2 + 1.5^2)$

(k) $\dfrac{8^2 - 5^2}{8 - 5}$

(l) $\dfrac{5.6^2 - 3.2^2}{5.6 - 3.2}$

*4 Can you spot a quick way to get the answer in 3 (k) and (l) above?
Try with some other numbers. Does it always work?

Sections F and G

1 Evaluate each of these expressions.

(a) $\sqrt{22.09} - 19.2$

(b) $\sqrt{22.09 - 19.2}$

(c) $\sqrt{29.16 \times 9.61}$

(d) $\dfrac{37.52 + 17.77}{\sqrt{28.09 + 4.4}}$

(e) $24.7 + \dfrac{11.2}{\sqrt{7.84}}$

(f) $\dfrac{\sqrt{10.24 + 6.57}}{1.52 - 0.88}$

2 Evaluate these.

(a) $3.1 - 2.4 \times {}^-1.2$

(b) $10.8 \times (3.7 - 8)$

(c) $21^2 - (4 \times {}^-5)$

(d) $({}^-4 \times 7)^2 - 81$

(e) $(3 + {}^-5.5) \times (13 - {}^-2.7)$

(f) $\dfrac{{}^-12}{2.4} - 2.7$

(g) $\dfrac{({}^-6 + 3.5)^2}{1.25}$

(h) $\dfrac{{}^-18 + 21^2}{(7 - {}^-3)^2 - 6}$

(i) $\dfrac{{}^-4.2 - 6}{{}^-5 + 3.3}$

(j) $\left(\dfrac{{}^-47}{5}\right)^2 - 10.3$

(k) $\dfrac{4.6^2 - 1}{1.6^2 - 0.16}$

*3 Copy and complete this cross-number puzzle. Write decimal points on the lines between squares.

$a = 5.6 \qquad b = {}^-10.5 \qquad c = {}^-6.3$

$d = {}^-0.64 \quad e = 4.8 \qquad f = 2.142$

$g = 62.8$

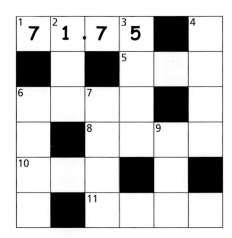

Across

1 $a + bc$

5 $\dfrac{ac}{b}$

6 $b + c^2$

8 bc

10 $c - \dfrac{a}{d}$

11 $e - ad$

Down

2 $\sqrt{a^2 + b^2}$

3 $a + \dfrac{f}{b}$

4 $\dfrac{b + c}{d}$

6 $a + de$

7 $2c^2 - g$

9 $\sqrt{b^2 - c^2} + \tfrac{1}{2}e$

Three dimensions

Section B

1 This shape is made with six cubes.

This is the front view.

(a) Draw a side view.

(b) Draw a top view.

2 This object is made from children's building blocks.

Draw three views of the object.

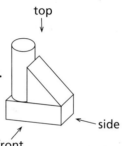

3 Draw a view of this object looking in the direction of each of the arrows A, B and C.

Section C

1 Calculate the volume of each of these cuboids.

(a) 6.5 cm by 8 cm by 4 cm   (b) 7.5 cm by 9 cm by 10 cm

(c) 16 cm by 12.5 cm by 8.5 cm   (d) 4.5 cm by 12 cm by 3.5 cm

2 The volume of each of these cuboids is 30 cm³.
Find the missing lengths.
(All dimensions are in cm.)

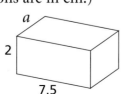

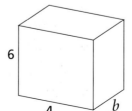

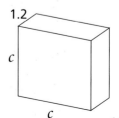

3 (a) A cube with sides 1 m long has a volume of 1 m^3.
How many cm^3 are there in 1 m^3?

(b) 1 litre = 1000 cm^3
How many litres are there in 1 m^3?

(c) How many litres of water does this
swimming pool hold when full?

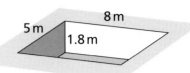

Section E

1 Here are some pictures
of prisms.
Each prism is made from
centimetre cubes or parts of them.

Work out the volume of each prism.

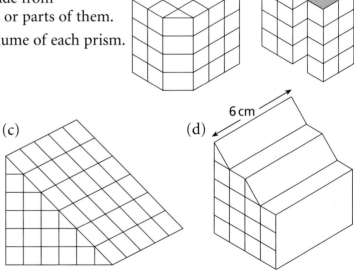

2 Calculate the
volume of each
of these prisms.

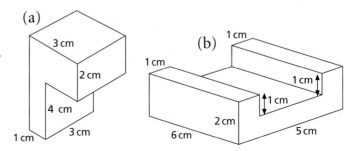

3 Calculate the volume of each of these triangular prisms.

(a)
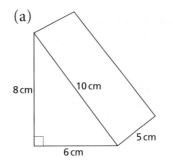

(b)
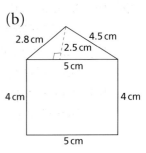

4 Calculate the volume of each of these prisms.

(a)
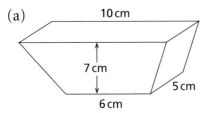

(b)
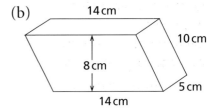

5 A patio is made by pouring $10\,\text{m}^3$ of concrete to cover an area of $42\,\text{m}^2$ to the same depth all over.

What is the depth of the concrete, in cm (to the nearest cm)?

6 Each of these prisms has a volume of $60\,\text{cm}^3$. Work out the missing dimensions.

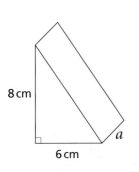

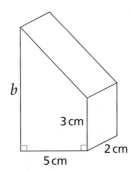

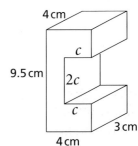

Section F

1 This cube has a spot on the front and a spot on the back. All the other faces are plain.

Copy and complete these nets of the cube.

(a)   (b)   (c)   (d)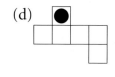

2 On a dice the numbers on opposite faces total 7. Copy this net of a dice. Find all the different ways of numbering the faces.

How many different dice are there?

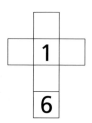

3 This cube has a square on three faces. All the other faces are plain.

Which of these diagrams are nets of the cube?

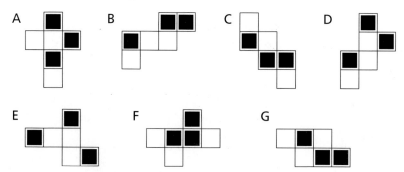

4 The nets of these solids are incomplete.
Sketch the incomplete nets and show the possible
positions for the missing face.

(a) 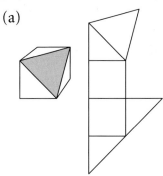 (b)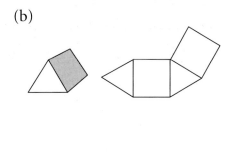

5 Here are the nets of some solids.
Sketch the solids.

(a)   (b)  (c)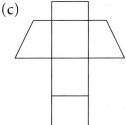

6 Each of these nets has one face missing.
What shape is the missing face?

(a) 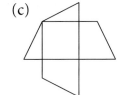 (b)

(c) 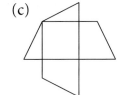 (d)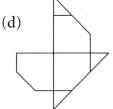

Section G

1 This is the net of a cuboid.

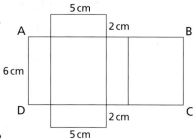

(a) What is the length AB?

(b) What is the area of rectangle ABCD?

(c) What is the surface area of the cuboid?

2 Find the surface area of each of these cuboids.

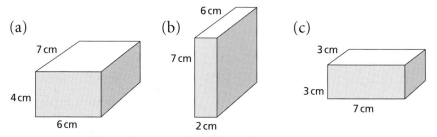

(a)

(b)

(c)

3 This solid ...

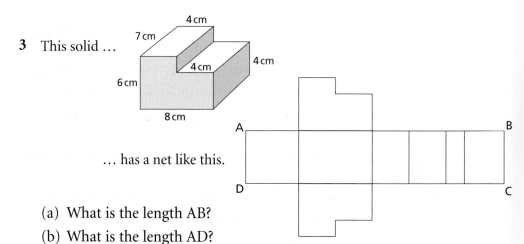

... has a net like this.

(a) What is the length AB?

(b) What is the length AD?

(c) What is the area of rectangle ABCD?

(d) What is the surface area of the solid?

106

4 Find the surface area of each of these solids.
All the measurements are in centimetres.

(a)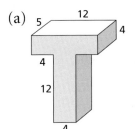

(b)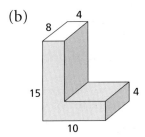

(c)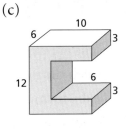

5 (a) What is the surface area of each of these cubes?

(i)   (ii) 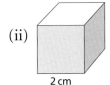   (iii)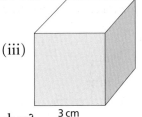

(b) What is the volume of each of these cubes?

(c) What are the surface area and the volume of the next cube in the sequence?

(d) What are the surface area and volume of a 12 cm cube?

6 In each pair of cuboids below, the dimensions of the second cuboid are double those of the first.
Find the surface areas of each pair of cuboids. What do you notice?

(a) (i) 3 cm by 5 cm by 4 cm   (ii) 6 cm by 10 cm by 8 cm

(b) (i) 1 cm by 3 cm by 8 cm   (ii) 2 cm by 6 cm by 16 cm

7 In each pair of cuboids below, the dimensions of the second cuboid are three times those of the first.
Find the surface areas of each pair of cuboids. What do you notice?

(a) (i) 1 cm by 5 cm by 5 cm   (ii) 3 cm by 15 cm by 15 cm

(b) (i) 1 cm by 2 cm by 6 cm   (ii) 3 cm by 6 cm by 18 cm

Finding formulas

Sections A and B

These designs are made from lines and dots. For each design,

    (a) sketch the next pattern

    (b) find a formula for the number of dots in pattern n

    (c) find a formula for the number of lines in pattern n

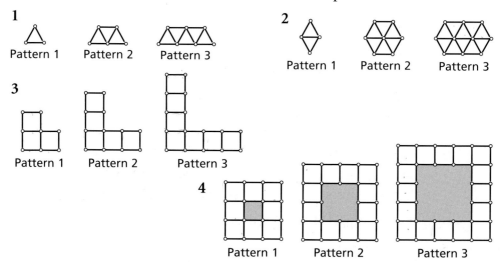

Sections C and D

1 For each of the following sequences,

    (i) describe a rule to go from one term to the next

    (ii) find the 10th term

(a) 3, 6, 12, 24, 48, ...   (b) 1, 5, 6, 11, 17, ...

(c) 94, 96, 98, 100, 102, ...   (d) 10, 11, 13, 16, 20, ...

(e) 25, 23, 21, 19, 17, ...   (f) 1, 2, 5, 14, 41, ...

2   Each expression below gives the nth term of a sequence.
    For each one,
    (i) find the first eight terms of the sequence
    (ii) decide whether the sequence is linear
    (iii) work out the 50th term

(a) $3n$ (b) $n - 3$ (c) $10 - n$

(d) $n^2 + 5$ (e) $2n + 4$ (f) $\frac{42}{n}$

Section E

1   For each of the following linear sequences,
    (i) find an expression for the nth term
    (ii) calculate the 100th term

(a) 7, 10, 13, 16, 19, ...   (b) 7, 12, 17, 22, 27, ...
(c) 3, 10, 17, 24, 31, ...   (d) 0, 5, 10, 15, 20, ...
(e) ⁻1, 5, 11, 17, 23, ...   (f) 5, 5.75, 6.5, 7.25, 8, ...

2   For each of the following linear sequences,
    (i) find the missing terms
    (ii) find an expression for the nth term
    (iii) calculate the 25th term

(a) 9, __ , __ , 15, ...   (b) 2, __ , __ , 26, ...

(c) ⁻1, __ , 5, __ , ...   (d) __ , 3, __ , 13, ...

3   I am a linear sequence. My 1st term is 7. My 5th term is 23.
    (a) Write down the 2nd, 3rd and 4th terms.
    (b) Find an expression for the nth term.

4   For the linear sequence 11, 15, 19, 23, ... , which term is 115?

5 Ben has £40 birthday money.
Each week he adds £2.50 to his money
so after 1 week he has saved £42.50.

(a) How much will he have saved after 3 weeks?

(b) Find an expression for the amount saved after n weeks.

(c) How much money will he have saved after 15 weeks?

(d) How many weeks will it take to save £100?

Section F

1 For each of the following linear sequences,

    (i) find an expression for the nth term

    (ii) calculate the 20th term

(a) 48, 46, 44, 42, 40, ...   (b) 20, 19, 18, 17, 16, ...

(c) 100, 95, 90, 85, 80, ...   (d) 7, 4, 1, ⁻2, ⁻5, ...

2 For each of the following linear sequences,

    (i) find the missing terms

    (ii) find an expression for the nth term

    (iii) calculate the 30th term

(a) 6, __ , __ , 0, ...   (b) 15, __ , __ , 12, ...

(c) ⁻2, __ , ⁻8, __ , ...   (d) __ , 34, __ , 18 ...

3 For each of the following linear sequences,

    (i) find an expression for the nth term

    (ii) calculate the 100th term

(a) ⁻3, 1, 5, 9, 13, ...   (b) 8, 7, 6, 5, 4, ...

(c) 14, 18, 22, 26, 30, ...   (d) 10, 25, 40, 55, 70, ...

(e) 8, 6, 4, 2, 0, ...   (f) 19.5, 19, 18.5, 18, 17.5, ...

39 Ratio

Section B

1   Most gold used for jewellery is a mixture of
    pure gold and other metals.
    18 carat gold is made by mixing 3 parts of
    pure gold with 1 part of other metals by weight.

    (a) How many grams of pure gold would you mix with:

        (i) 5 g of other metals   (ii) 12 g of other metals

    (b) How many grams of other metals would you mix with

        (i) 30 g of gold   (ii) 42 g of gold

2   Here is a recipe for 9 carat gold.
    Copy and complete the table.

Mix 3 parts of pure gold
with 5 parts of other metals.

Pure gold (g)	Other metals (g)
6	
12	
15	
	15
	30
	75

3   Here is the recipe for 22 carat gold.

    Mix 33 parts of gold with 2 parts of silver
    and 1 part of copper by weight.

    (a) How much silver and how much copper would you mix
        with 99 g of pure gold?

    (b) How much copper and how much gold would you mix
        with 20 g of silver?

    (c) How much gold and how much copper would you mix
        with 30 g of silver?

Section D

1 Amy made a necklace using 24 red beads and 18 green beads.

    (a) Write the ratio of red beads to green beads in its simplest form.

    (b) Write the ratio of green beads to red beads in its simplest form.

2 Write each of these ratios in its simplest form.

    (a) 4:6   (b) 12:4   (c) 15:25   (d) 15:6   (e) 21:18

3 Copy and complete these so that all the ratios in each group are equal.

    (a) 2:3   ☐:9   10:☐   (b) 4:1   ☐:3   8:☐

    (c) 6:2   ☐:1   18:☐   (d) 4:10   2:☐   ☐:15

    (e) 30:40 ☐:8   3:☐   (f) 7:3   21:☐   ☐:12

4 Match each ratio from group A with an equal ratio from group B.

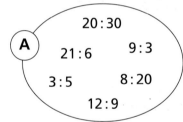 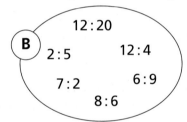

5 A compost for growing cacti is made by mixing loam and sand in the ratio of 3:1.

    (a) How many bags of loam go with 3 bags of sand?

    (b) How many bags of sand go with 12 bags of loam?

    (c) How many bags of loam and how many bags of sand are needed to make 20 bags of cacti compost?

6 Purple paint is made by mixing blue and red in the ratio of 3:2.

    (a) How many litres of red paint go with 6 litres of blue paint?

    (b) How many litres of blue paint go with 8 litres of red paint?

    (c) How many litres of blue paint and how many litres of red paint are needed to make 25 litres of purple paint?

Section E

1 Tony's class were going to raise some money for charity.
   They decided to share it between two charities in the ratio of 2:3.

   Write down how much each charity would receive if the class raised

   (a) £10   (b) £25   (c) £80   (d) £42.50

2 Paul and Anna are being paid £30 to do some gardening.
   They decide to share the payment according to
   how many hours they work.

   (a) How much is Anna's share if she
       works for 2 hours and
       Paul works for 4 hours?

   (b) What is Paul's share if he
       works for 2 hours and
       Anna works for 3 hours?

   (c) How much do they each get if
       Paul works for 5 hours and
       Anna works for 3 hours?

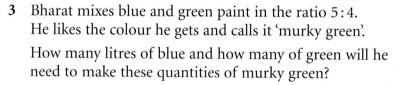

3 Bharat mixes blue and green paint in the ratio 5:4.
   He likes the colour he gets and calls it 'murky green'.

   How many litres of blue and how many of green will he
   need to make these quantities of murky green?

   (a) 36 litres   (b) 13.5 litres   (c) 17.1 litres

4 Share £120 in the ratio
   (a) 1:2:3   (b) 2:1:2   (c) 2:3:5   (d) 2:3:7

5 Share £3.50 in the ratio
   (a) 1:2:4   (b) 2:3:5   (c) 3:5:6   (d) 10:12:13

Section F

1   Each of these patterns continues in all directions.

What is the ratio of grey triangles to white triangles in each pattern?

(a)

(b)

(c)

(d)

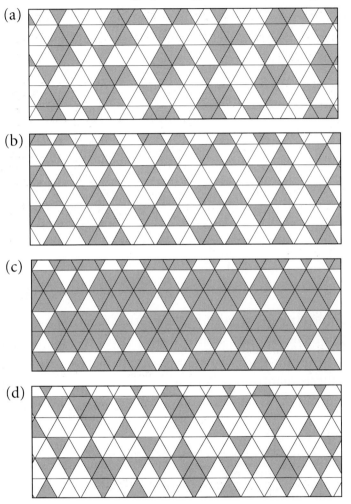

2   Using triangular dotty paper, design a tiling with grey and white tiles in the ratio $3:2$.

Section G

1 A shop sells two different writing sets.

Set A contains 40 sheets of paper and 15 envelopes.

Set B contains 25 sheets of paper and 9 envelopes.

Which set has the higher ratio of sheets to envelopes?
Explain how you decide.

2 Different types of pastry use different amounts of flour and fat in their recipes.

The table shows the flour and butter content for five pastries.

Write the names of the pastries in order starting with the pastry with the highest ratio of flour to butter.

Pastry	Flour (g)	Butter (g)
Flan	100	75
Flaky	225	175
Rough puff	225	150
Choux	65	50
Puff	450	450

Section H

1 These rectangles are made by adding a square to the longest side of the previous rectangle.

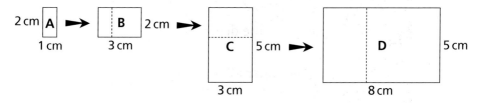

(a) What are the sizes of the next three rectangles?

(b) Calculate the ratio $\dfrac{\text{long side}}{\text{short side}}$ for each rectangle.

(c) What do you notice about your answers?
Investigate for more rectangles.

Functions and graphs

Section A

1   A swimming pool contains water to a depth of 80 cm.
    A hose is turned on and the depth increases 20 cm in each minute.

    (a) Copy and complete this table showing the depth, d cm, after the
        hose has been on for t minutes.

t	0	1	2	3	4	5
d	80	100				

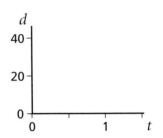

    (b) Find the formula connecting t and d.
        Write it in the form $d = \ldots$

    (c) Draw a graph from the table.
        Use the scales shown here.

    (d) Use the graph to find the value of t for
        which $d = 128$.

2   Mika has made a 'water clock'. It consists of a tall
    container with a tiny hole in the base, through which
    water leaks out slowly.

    When she starts the clock, the depth of the water in
    the container is 30 cm.

    The depth, d cm, of the water after t minutes is given
    by the formula $d = 30 - 4t$

    (a) Copy and complete this table.

t	0	1	2	3	4	5
d	30					

    (b) Draw a graph from the table.
        Label it '$d = 30 - 4t$'.

    (c) Use the graph to find after how many minutes
        the water is 16 cm deep.

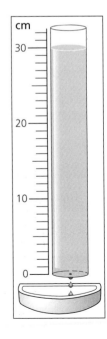

Sections B and C

1 (a) Make a table of values for the function $y = 2x - 4$
      for values of x from ⁻4 to 4.

   (b) Draw and label the graph of $y = 2x - 4$.

2 (a) Make a table of values for the function $y = 9 - 2x$
      for values of x from ⁻4 to 4.

   (b) Draw and label the graph of $y = 9 - 2x$.

3 Find the equation of
   each line shown here.

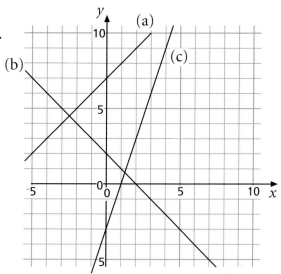

4 Sean did an experiment with a bed
   spring. He put different weights on
   it and measured its height.

   He drew this graph of his results.

   Find a formula linking h and w.

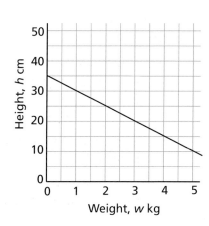

Mixed questions 5

1   ABCD is a cross-section of a motorway cutting.

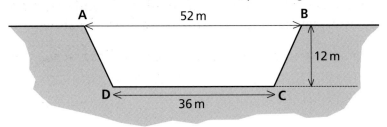

(a) Calculate the area of the cross-section.

(b) The cutting is 120 m long and has the same cross-section along its length. Calculate the volume of earth that was removed when the cutting was made.

(c) The removed earth was carried away in lorries, each holding 82.5 m³. How many lorry loads were carried?

2   These objects are made by glueing 1 cm cubes together.

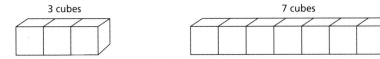

(a) Calculate the surface area of each of the objects shown above.

(b) Find a formula for the surface area of the object with n cubes.

(c) One of these objects has a surface area of 150 cm².
How many cubes is it made from?

(d) This cross shape is made so that there are two cubes in each 'arm'.
Find a formula for the surface area of a cross shape with n cubes in each arm.

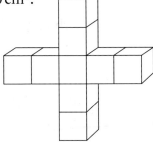

3 Ann is 3 years old, Brian is 4 and Charlie is 5.

(a) Their aunt gives them £30 and they agree to share it in the ratio of their ages. How much does each of them get?

(b) A year later, their aunt gives them another £30 and they have the same agreement. How much does each get this time?

4 Find a formula for the nth term of each of these linear sequences.

(a) 2, 5, 8, 11, 14, 17, ...

(b) ⁻7, ⁻3, 1, 5, 9, 13, ...

(c) 26, 24, 22, 20, 18, ...

(d) 5, ⁻4, ⁻13, ⁻22, ⁻27, ...

5 Find the equation of each of the graphs shown below.

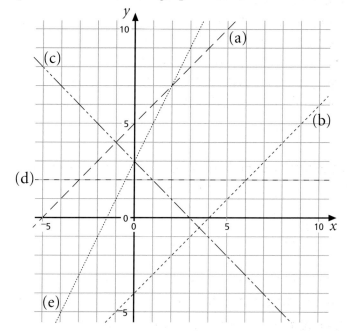

6 For each graph in question 5, work out the value of y when x is

(i) 100   (ii) ⁻100

7 Use a calculator to calculate (a) $\dfrac{8.05 - 1.85}{(4.7 - 3.2)^2}$ (b) $3.69 + \dfrac{\sqrt{1.69}}{5.2 \times 1.6}$

Give your answers correct to two decimal places.

8 A metallic mixture is made by mixing copper, iron and tin in the ratio $3:4:5$ by weight.

Calculate what percentage of the mixture is copper.

9 Manoj counted the number of people (including the driver) in cars entering the town centre one morning.
Here is a summary of his results.

Number of people in car	1	2	3	4	5	6
Frequency	26	18	14	10	7	2

(a) Find the modal number of people in a car.

(b) Find the median number of people in a car.

(c) Find the mean number of people in a car, to two decimal places.

10 The 10th term of a linear sequence is 40.
The 3rd term is $^-16$.

Find (a) the first term   (b) an expression for the nth term

11 Dawn has three pairs of gloves in her drawer, a red pair, a blue pair and a green pair.
Each pair consists of a left-hand and a right-hand glove.
The gloves are all mixed up and she takes out two gloves at random.

(a) Make a list of all the possible outcomes (for example, she could take the red left hand and the blue left hand).

(b) What is the probability that she takes out a left-hand and a right-hand glove?

(c) What is the probability that she takes out a pair of the same colour?

*12 Rajesh makes green paint by mixing blue and yellow in the ratio $1:3$. Jane makes a lighter green by mixing blue and yellow in the ratio $1:4$.

Colin takes a litre of Rajesh's green paint and a litre of Jane's and mixes them together.
What is the ratio of blue to yellow in Colin's mixture?
(It is **not** $2:7$!)